# TOMB KINGS

A WARHAMMER ARMIES SUPPLEMENT

# CONTENTS



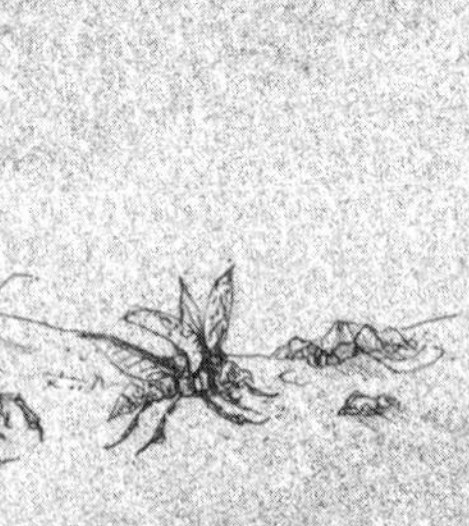


**Army List Design**
Alessio Cavatore

**Development**
Anthony Reynolds
& Gav Thorpe

**Additional Material**
Space McQuirk
& Graham McNeill

**Illustrations**
John Blanche, Alex Boyd,
Paul Dainton, David Gallagher,
Nuala Kennedy & Karl Kopinski

**Cover Illustration**
Paul Dainton

**Graphics**
Nuala Kennedy
& Stefan Kopinski

**Production**
Dylan Owen & Nathan Winter

**Miniatures Designers**
Dave Andrews, Juan Diaz,
Colin Dixon, Colin Grayson,
Mark Harrison, Alex Hedström,
Aly Morrison & Trish Morrison

**Model Makers**
Mark Jones & Dave Andrews

**Miniatures Painters**
Neil Green, Tammy Haye,
Darren Latham, Kirsten Mickleburgh,
Seb Perbet & Keith Robertson

**Thanks also to**
Gordon Davidson, Glenn Ford,
Chris Frosin, Jes Goodwin,
Gareth Hamilton, Mark Havener,
Mark Hopko, Phil Kelly, Dave Lawrence,
Adrian McWalter, Pete Scholey,
Andrew Sinclair & Joe Sleboda

PRODUCED BY GAMES WORKSHOP





*British cataloguing-in-Publication Data. A catalogue record for this book is available from the British Library.*



| UK | US | Australia | Canada | Japan |
|---|---|---|---|---|
| Games Workshop, | Games Workshop, | Games Workshop, | 2679 Bristol Circle, | Games Workshop, |
| Willow Rd, Lenton, | 6721 Baymeadow Drive, | 23 Liverpool Street, | Units 2&3, | Willow Rd, Lenton, |
| Nottingham, | Glen Burnie, | Ingleburn | Oakville, | Nottingham, |
| NG7 2WS | Maryland, 21060-6401 | NSW 2565 | Ontario, L6H 6Z8 | NG7 2WS, UK |



**ISBN: 1-84154-336-5** **www.games-workshop.com** **Product Code: 60 03 02 07 003**

# INTRODUCTION

The ancient realm of Nehekhara was once the greatest civilisation of Men in the world, but hundreds of years before the rise of Sigmar the treachery of the Great Necromancer, Nagash, almost destroyed and enslaved this mighty realm. Brought back to immortal unlife by arcane magic, the Tomb Kings of Nehekhara continue to lead their Undead armies, fighting to protect their mighty empire from the depredations of the lesser races and expand their dominion even further.

The Tomb Kings army has a unique playing style. At face value, its troops seem expensive, slow and not very good in combat. However, when bolstered by the considerable fighting abilities of the Tomb Kings and Princes, and animated by the incantations of the Liche Priests, they can be used in devastating combinations to shatter the enemy. The Tomb Kings are an army that rewards a meticulous approach to army selection and planning. Careful coordination of your units, magic and magic items can turn a ramshackle collection of bones into a highly disciplined, deadly force.

The spectacle of a Tomb Kings army on the battlefield is one of the most dazzling in Warhammer. Ranks upon ranks of gleaming bone, decorated with bronze and gold, is a marvellous sight and an intimidating one for your opponents. A few simple painting techniques are all you need to get a battle-worthy force ready in a short time. If you can paint bones, then you can paint a Tomb Kings army!

In this book you will find:

**The Rise of Nehekhara.** The ancient history of Nehekhara, descriptions and maps of the realms of the Tomb Kings and other background information.

**Legions of the Tomb Kings.** Full details and rules for the characters, warriors, monsters and war machines of the Tomb Kings army. Also, rules for the unique Liche Priest Incantations, and a full range of magical artifacts with which to equip your mighty heroes.

**Armies of Khemri.** A full list of all the different troop types in the Tomb Kings force, enabling you to field your army in games of Warhammer.

**Lords of Nehekhara.** Details of two of the most infamous rulers from the Land of the Dead – almighty Settra, Tomb King of Khemri and High Queen Khalida Nerferher.

**The Land of the Dead.** More background information, tactical advice for Tomb Kings generals and a summary of the Tomb Kings rules.

## LEGENDARY KINGS OF NEHEKHARA

Before the time when Settra prevailed over them, there were many kings in many places and their names are not remembered, save for NEHEK of whom it is said that in his time no one lived in cities. Then afterwards came ZAKASH who was king in Zandri. In his time, it is said, writing was invented. Then came many kings until the time of KHESEK who subjugated the desert dwellers and founded Numas. Then after him came HEKESH. He made war on many kings. Thereafter there was strife in the land. With the coming of Settra, the great rulership of Khemri became as law. Here be a record of the kings of blessed Khemri.

## THE DYNASTIES OF KHEMRI

### 1st DYNASTY

**SETTRA**

[C -2500 Imperial Calendar]

So it is said of Settra: He conquered the entire land of Nehekhara from the mountains to the sea. He levied tribute upon all the people of the great river. He appointed princes and bound them under his rule. He founded the mighty city of Khemri as his residence. His wealth and power was great. His heart was vexed that he should be mortal and die. Therefore did he establish the Priesthood of the Awakening and caused to be built a Pyramid of Eternity. He was the first king to be wrapped for his awakening to his reign of millions of years.

**AHTAF I**

So it is said of Ahtaf: He desired a pyramid as great as that of his father but half the kingdom rebelled against him. The prince of Zandri and the prince of Numas raised themselves up as kings.

**KHUTEF**

So it is said of Khutef: He made strong the kingdom and did not pay tribute to any king.

**AHTAF II**

So it is said of Ahtaf: He caused to be built a strong fleet of ships.

**UTEP**

So it is said of Utep: In his time the priests learned great secrets and did not die.

**WAKHAF**

So it is said of Wakhaf: In his time the desert dwellers were repelled.

**SEKHEF**

So it is said of Sekhef: He caused discord among the priests.

**NEKHESH**

So it is said of Nekhesh: In his time there was strife in the Necropolis.

# THE RISE OF NEHEKHARA

Countless centuries ago in the land of Nehekhara, far to the south of the Old World, there rose a mighty civilisation of Man. It was at its most powerful two and a half millennia before the coming of the barbaric hero-deity Sigmar, a time when the other Men of the world were still primitive and savage. The ancient myths and legends of these people, carved on the tombs and monuments of their cities, say that the Nehekharans were so favoured by the heavens that the first of them were nurtured and taught by the gods themselves. Greatest of the cities of Nehekhara was Khemri. The other cities were each ruled and governed by their own kings, though they all were loyal and paid tribute to the king of Khemri itself. Together, these kings conquered the tribes in the surrounding lands, drove back the greenskins and ruled from the western desert to the eastern sea. At the height of their power they had expanded and conquered lands as far north as what is now the Empire, far south into the steaming jungle of the Southlands as well as to the north and east into the Dark Lands. Their fleets of war galleys terrorised the Great Ocean, raiding up and down the coast and causing terror wherever they went.

# THE LEGACY OF KING SETTRA

It was Settra, the first Priest King of Khemri, who conquered the other Kings, making Khemri the pre-eminent city of Nehekhara and beginning the golden age of his kingdom. He was a powerful warrior and a mighty leader, feared across half the world. Rather than taking satisfaction in his successes, Settra was aggrieved that death would one day rob him of his lands and power. Determined to overcome this intolerable situation, he ordered his priests to find a way to ensure that he would live forever. Settra was consumed with his quest to find immortality and to live in the paradise he had created for all eternity.

The priests of Khemri did as Settra bade them, and for years they brewed potions and recited incantations determined to decipher the riddle of everlasting life. They travelled into unknown lands in search of the secret that would overcome death. In their research, the priests learned much but soon realised that true immortality lay beyond their power. They were naturally reluctant to reveal these limitations to their King and continued to search for the secret of eternal life, though they held little hope of discovering it. The priests wisely decided to keep some of what they discovered to themselves. By means of incantations learnt through mysterious and ancient sources, the priests used their knowledge to extend their own lives for centuries. Nevertheless, they could not halt the passage of time indefinitely and were merely postponing the inevitability of death while their bodies became frail and withered.

# THE PYRAMID OF SETTRA

Despite the best efforts of the priests, Settra could not be saved from death. When Settra finally perished, full of anger and pride to his last breath, powerful incantations were intoned over his body and he was embalmed with great ritual. Preserved against decay, the body of Settra was entombed deep beneath the earth under a mighty pyramid of shining white stone. The Liche Priests of Khemri had never discovered a way of avoiding death but they believed that with proper magic and careful preparation it might be possible for the dead to eventually return to life in imperishable bodies. The Liche Priests told Settra this as he lay dying, promising him eternal life upon his awakening. For thousands of years afterwards they and their kind tended the flames in his tomb, nurturing his spirit with sacrifice and magic in preparation for the day of awakening. Their lives extended long beyond those of other mortal men and, because of their longevity and unsurpassed wisdom, the Liche Priests of Khemri enjoyed dominion over the land of Nehekhara second only to that of the Kings themselves.

# THE TIME OF THE KINGS

After Settra came many kings, though there was never one as powerful or influential. Upon their death, these too were entombed within towering pyramids to await when they would reawaken into paradise. Over time, the shining cities of the dead outgrew the meagre cities of the living – all the efforts of the people were expended in building and maintaining the tombs of the Kings, and the entire culture of Nehekhara came to revolve around preparing the way to their reawakening. Soon lesser nobles demanded similar rites and their tombs were built alongside the royal pyramids. Throughout the whole land of Nehekhara, monuments of the dead rose above the cities of the living.

This long age was a time of prosperity for Nehekhara. Armies of chariots, strong bowmen and highly disciplined warriors marched to war against each of the Kings' enemies. In the west the crude desert nomads were subjugated and their chieftains forced to send tribute to Khemri in the form of slaves, gold, and precious stones. In the north and south the Kings fought many battles against tribes of greenskins and barbaric men. These wars brought much wealth and many exotic materials to build the royal tombs. None could stand against the might of Nehekhara and they ruled supreme across the lands. However, tragedy struck the Nehekharans, and the entire society was soon to be destroyed by one man.

## 2nd DYNASTY

### RAKAPH I

So it is said of Rakaph: He pacified the land of Khemri and restored the priests of the former kings.

### RAKHASH

So it is said of Rakhash: He desired much gold. He led a mighty army beyond the mountains. He established the stronghold of Rasetra. He received the tribute of the lands of Mahrak, Lybaras and Lahmia.

### RAKAPH II

So it is said of Rakaph: He subjugated the lands of Mahrak, Lybaras and Lahmia and placed princes over them.

### PHARAKH

So it is said of Pharakh: He caused to be dug the Canal of Abundance. Ten thousand laboured for ten years and the land prospered exceedingly. Mighty was his pyramid in the Necropolis.

### RAKAPH III

So it is said of Rakaph: He reigned for many years so that no prince lived to succeed him. In his time the desert dwellers were repelled on three occasions.

### QUEEN RASUT

So it is said of Queen Rasut: She seized the throne for herself, so that no king of Zandri or Numas should reign in Khemri. None dared oppose her. She exhalted the priests and rewarded the soldiers. Her infant son was placed upon the throne on her demise but he did not live to see his third year.

## 3rd DYNASTY

### KHETEP

So it is said of Khetep: He was the regent of Queen Rasut's infant son, and he took the throne upon his death. He caused to be built the Great Pyramid which is in the Necropolis of Khemri. One million slaves laboured for twenty five years upon the orders of the king. All kings fell upon their knees before Khetep in his time. The land of Nehekhara prospered as never before.

### THUTEP

So it is said of Thutep: He was entombed in the Great Pyramid of Khetep, his father, while yet alive and the throne was seized by his brother.

### NAGASH

So it is said of Nagash the Accursed One, foremost among priests and greatest in learning: He seized the throne of Khemri from the rightful king, his brother. Arkhan was his Vizier. He caused the third part of the priests of the Necropolis to turn from their former ways. He caused to be built the Black Pyramid which is in the Necropolis of Khemri. Innumerable slaves toiled for fifty years upon his orders. He was overthrown by the army of the Seven Kings.

## 4th DYNASTY

LAHMIZZAR

So it is said of Lahmizzar, King of Lahmia: He began the war against Nagash and caused the kings of Zandri, Numas, Mahrak, Lybaras and Rasetra to follow him. He was slain at the hand of Nagash.

LAHMIZZASH

So it is said of Lahmizzash: He continued the war against Nagash and led the other kings and besieged Khemri. He caused Khemri to be sacked. He caused Nagash to flee and Arkhan to be slain and the Great Necropolis to be desecrated. He purged the priesthood. He caused the name of Nagash to be struck from inscriptions. At this time, the beloved of Nehekhara, Queen Khalida Neferher, was slain in the court of the Lahmians, and their dark secret remained undiscovered.

LAKHASHAR

So it is said of Lakhashar: He ruled Khemri.

LAHKASHAZ

So it is said of Lakhashaz: He ruled as king in Khemri. In his time, the kings of Zandri, Numas, Mahrak, Lybaras and Rasetra made war on each other and there was rebellion in Khemri. The king was defeated and slain.

## 5th DYNASTY

SETEP

So it is said of Setep: He made himself king of Khemri. He restored the Necropolis and replenished the priesthood.

## 6th DYNASTY

ALKHAZZAR I

So it is said of Alkhazzar: He was the general of King Setep. The king made him his heir so that he ascended to the kingdom. He caused to be raised a mighty host of chariots. In his time Numas was subjugated.

ALKHAZZAR II

So it is said of Alkhazzar: He marched against Zandri and received its tribute. He caused the desert dwellers to fear Khemri.

ALKHARAD

So it is said of Alkharad: He fought against Mahrak and Lybaras and brought Rasetra under his rule. He received the tribute of unknown tribes.

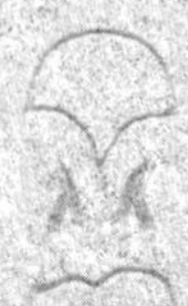

# THE TREACHERY OF NAGASH

The fall of the land of Nehekhara and the tragic destruction of its people was brought about by the ambition of a single, twisted sorcerer. Once he held the honoured position of high priest of Khemri, yet he began to corrupt the religious incantations of the order of priests and betrayed the king of Khemri, his own brother. Filled with greed and pride, Nagash coveted the throne held by his brother and set into motion a plan to become king as well as high priest. One night, as the clouds covered the moon, he murdered the young king, entombing him alive within the Great Pyramid of Khetep. The next morning, blood still staining his hands, he placed himself on the throne and none dared confront him.

The reign of Nagash was a time of terror for all the people of Nehekhara. The usurper king sought to increase his own power by means of devilish sorcery, a blasphemy that the people of Nehekhara felt certain would incur the wrath of the gods. He conjured evil daemons to do his bidding and learned many dark secrets in this way. In order to build his own tomb he demanded great quantities of gold and slaves to be sent in tribute to Khemri. Stone the colour of ebony was brought from afar and soon the Black Pyramid of Nagash towered above all others, rising hundreds of metres into the sky. So great was the tribute brutally exacted by Nagash that starvation wracked the lands and the great cities fell into ruin. Eventually the Kings of the other cities of Nehekhara rallied against Nagash and their armies attacked Khemri.

The Priest-King Nagash used his infernal powers to raise a legion of long-dead warriors. This was the first time that the dead were made to walk at the will of another, and the horror of it caused many to flee before the undead armies.

After a titanic battle, Nagash was eventually defeated. Some thought him destroyed, yet he managed to escape to the north-east to plot his revenge. The cursed Black Pyramid was abandoned and for centuries it remained a haunted place shunned by all.

For hundreds of years the kings continued to rule Nehekhara, yet the corruption of Nagash had tarnished the royal line of Khemri and his treachery was never forgotten. His blasphemous dabbling in cursed sorceries spread to the city of Lahmia whose queen embraced the malign magic and consorted with daemonic powers. She had drunk from the elixir of Nagash, extending her life indefinitely yet cursing her for all eternity. Fearful of the wrath of the gods, King Alcadizaar made war on the tainted queen, leading a massed army against Lahmia. Hundreds of chariots raced across the land ahead of mighty phalanxes of archers and spearmen. The might of Lahmia was smashed, and the queen fled, accompanied by those she had embraced into her cursed vampiric existence.

Nagash, who had managed to escape destruction centuries earlier and was residing in the mountains to the north-east of Khemri recognised the spawn of his own ancient evil and was gladdened by the corruption of the lords of Lahmia. He welcomed them, and the vampires became his captains – fell creatures clad in dark shadows whose actions were guided by the strength of their master's will. Nagash sent the vampires to make war upon Khemri, and he vowed to turn the entire world into a kingdom of the dead. At their back came the dead warriors of a mighty army, skeletons drawn from their tombs by the power of Nagash's sorcery.

War and strife assailed Nehekhara for years on end and the land was irredeemably scarred, but Nagash underestimated his former countrymen. Alcadizaar the Conqueror was the greatest general of his age and led the unified army of Nehekhara against Nagash's evil for all the long years of battle. Finally, the undead hordes of Nagash were pushed back, yet the evil sorcerer himself still walked the land. His corrupt necromantic magic was still new and not yet perfected, and his power was not as great as it would later become.

ALCADIZAAR
THE CONQUEROR
[C -1200 Imperial Calendar]

So it is said of Alcadizaar the Conqueror: He bound the entire land of Nehekhara under his rule. The kings of Zandri, Numas, Mahrak, Lybaras and Rasetra offered up their tribute to him. He was a wise ruler so that there was great prosperity and rejoicing throughout the land. In his time, Nagash came against the land, but Alcadizaar, the king, prevailed against him. Cursed Lahmia was sacked and all the people were enslaved. Thereafter plague beset the entire land and the river flowed red with blood. Every living thing that was in the land suffered, and many died, save for the Liche Priests who are beyond death, and the land became desolate. Nehekhara became a land of the dead. Then Nagash came forth for a second time and the king could not prevail over him, because nine tenths of his people had perished and those who remained sickened unto death. Then the king was carried off in chains to the palace of Nagash. Thereupon Nagash wasted the land and awakened the kings resting in the Necropolis. However, it is said that in the darkness, Alcadizaar rose up and slew Nagash, saving the kings from forced servitude to cursed Nagash. Such was the greatness of Alcadizaar. Thus ends the living line of Khemrian kings.

## 7th DYNASTY
## THE AWAKENED ONES

SETTRA THE IMPERISHABLE
[C -1151 Imperial Calendar to present]

So it is said of Settra: He was awakened before his rest of millions of years was completed. He arose with his army and saw that his former realm was desolate. He made himself mighty over the other kings of former times which had awakened. He repelled Arkhan the Black who contended with him for rulership over Khemri. He contends against the awakened kings of Zandri and Numas so that they tremble at his name! Bitter civil war wracks the lands of Nehekhara, but he who was the first king of Khemri is to be its last for evermore. Mighty is he, and he overthrows the strongholds of the desert dwellers. Wise ruler who causes the gods to rejoice! He whose rule is everlasting!

### Annals Of The Reign Of Millions Of Years

Settra's Reign of Millions of Years is considered to have begun with his awakening approximately 1150 years before Sigmar, by the Imperial Reckoning. Thus Settra and the other Tomb Kings awakened at this time are in their 3500th year of their everlasting reigns. Many kings have awakened at various intervals since the great awakening, and thus date their reigns from that time. Needless to say, many awakened kings claim sovereignty over the same Necropoli and, when not actually at war with each other, remain in uneasy peace or temporary alliance.

The Liche Priests of Nehekhara have compiled annals of the reign of the awakened Settra since the beginning, and these are recorded on scrolls and also inscribed in hieroglyphic script on the walls of various restored temples in the Necropolis. What follows is a summary of the shortest of these annals. Only a selection of interesting events are included because they either refer to contact with other races or give an insight to what happens within Nehekhara. Note that Settra's year dates are used, and these should not to be confused with Imperial reckoning.

YEAR 1: The rising of Settra, the Awakened One. The king went forth against the accursed Arkhan causing him to flee into the uttermost wastes. The purging of the Necropolis on the orders of the king. The Nagashites were put to death except for those who escaped the wrath of the king.

YEAR 2: The acclamation of Settra, the king, as foremost among the Awakened Ones in the land of Nehekhara, and Lord of the Necropolis. The bringing of tribute from the Lords of Zandri, Numas and Rasetra.

YEAR 136: King Settra and King Rakash went forth to overthrow the rebels in the Necropolis of Mahrak.

YEAR 275: Strife in the Necropolis of Zandri.

YEAR 554: King Alkharad awakened and did battle against the Orchites and the Goblites in the Wall of Bones.

YEAR [illegible]: The Accursed One came forth from his tomb. He turned his face from the great might of Settra the Invincible, against whom he cannot prevail. Thereupon he went into Zandri and from there also into Numas, but the kings of these places harkened not to his evil words.

YEAR 1112: Arkhan went forth from the desert to follow his accursed lord. Thereupon Settra rose to do battle against the heretics. All the Tomb Kings followed Settra. Then the evil ones were pursued out of the land of Nehekhara and into the wilderness regions. When the Tomb Kings of Zandri and Numas saw that the might of Settra had prevailed over the evil ones, treachery entered their hearts. They fought against the mighty Settra for seven days and seven nights, but Settra prevailed against them. The rebels slunk back to their own tombs, knowing that Settra the Everlasting, is lord over Khemri and all of Nehekhara.

# THE VENGEANCE OF NAGASH

Such was Nagash's bitterness, so great the potency of his thwarted ambition, that he chose to end all life in Nehekhara rather than see anyone else hold power over the land. He polluted the clear water of the river Vitae, poisoning it until the water turned thick and dark, tainting the lands that relied on its life-bringing waters. Forever after, the river was known as the river Mortis. Pestilence spread rampantly across the land of Nehekhara and those who succumbed to the terrible plagues soon began to outnumber the living. Weeping for his lost people, Alcadizaar sat upon his throne as his kingdom was destroyed by a foe that he could not fight. He watched as his friends and advisors died, then his children and finally his wife Khalida, named after the revered Queen of Lybaras. As Nagash's undead forces once again attacked Nehekhara, there was only a meagre defence, for most of the population had already perished. Finally, Alcadizaar was captured and dragged away to rot in a dungeon cell beneath Nagash's fortress.

Filled with insane visions of power, Nagash began to cast the greatest and most terrifying spell he had ever conceived. As he chanted within his fortress to the north-east of Nehekhara, the sky for hundreds of miles began to darken and the ground shook. As his spell reached its crescendo, a great wave of power surged from the sorcerer's body, washing over the lands of Nehekhara and stealing the life from everything in its path. Crops shrivelled and animals perished within seconds. The last people of Nehekhara fell to the ground, their skin withering as if they had aged a century in the blink of an eye. Within minutes, there was not a single living creature in the entirety of Nehekhara. Nagash planned to raise the entire population of Nehekhara, an unstoppable army of the dead that he could use to conquer the world.

While Nagash was lost in his dreams of triumph and drained of power, Alcadizaar, the last living king of Nehekhara, was mysteriously freed from his prison by a group of hunched, heavily cloaked creatures. A powerful blade was pushed into his hands, and he stumbled into Nagash's throne room where the twisted sorcerer was recovering from his great expenditure of energy. A mighty battle ensued, and Nagash was eventually cut down by the last king of Khemri. Alcadizaar disappeared from the history books, filled with horror at the obscenities he had seen, and having witnessed the death of his beloved realm.

# THE KINGDOM OF THE DEAD

The only things that moved within the dead cities were the withered and ancient Liche Priests. Their bodies, already extended far beyond their natural life span, seemed to be unaffected by the curse of Nagash. Though they could not guess it yet, they had become immortal at last – though in a manner none could have foretold.

Nagash's foul magic penetrated the tombs of the kings and reverberated throughout the charnel pits of the dead city. His cruel spell affected these dead kings and their minions in a different manner, and they rose from their resting places. From long-forgotten crypts, skeleton warriors burst forth, ready to do their king's bidding. After centuries of entombment, the stiffened corpses of heroes and ancient generals stirred. While the skeletal warriors were little more than automatons awaiting their lords' directions, the kings and princes awoke from their long sleep of death with their memories and faculties intact due to the incantations of preservation performed on their embalmed bodies. They emerged from their tombs in horror. They had expected to arise resplendent from death into an eternal paradise, yet their bodies were little more than crumbling husks, their land was in ruin and their kingdoms shattered.

The ambition and pride that had driven the Nehekharan kings in life still resided in their ancient bodies, and they instantly set out to reclaim their empires as best as they could. There were hundreds of kings, for the tradition of embalming the dead had existed for countless generations and those who were great and powerful in life were now but one amongst many.

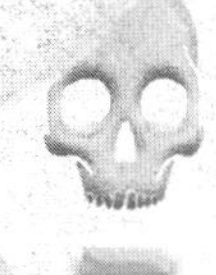

There were long battles in the necropoli amongst the kings, and thousands of skeleton warriors were destroyed. In Khemri, the battle between rival kings lasted for two days before the tomb of Settra opened and the King himself, first and mightiest of all the Kings of Nehekhara, marched from his resting place accompanied by thousands of his personal guard. He struck down dozens of lesser Tomb Kings, destroying them utterly, and his Tomb Guard overwhelmed all opposition. Before long the kings of Khemri bowed their heads to him, the greatest of all kings, and soon he had reconquered all of Nehekhara.

Settra commanded the surviving Liche Priests to explain to him why the awakening had gone awry before the right and proper time. The Liche Priests cowered before the outraged king and told the history of Nehekhara since his passing, over a thousand years previous. As best they could, they told Settra of the spell that the foul Nagash had cast, cursing Nehekhara for all time.

Settra listened with a controlled rage simmering within him. Once he had learned all he could from the Liche Priests he commanded that the Kings return to their eternal rest. The Liche Priests were expelled from his sight, for Settra in his vanity believed that his own powers far surpassed those of the Priests who had lied to him. They were given the duty of watching over the tombs and Nehekhara itself and to awake the kings as needed. Settra vowed that he would stay vigilant, taking stock of the world and waging war as was his wont. In particular, he would watch for the hated Nagash who had cursed him, for he knew that the necromancer might yet reappear in the world, and whose magic could still threaten his immortality.

So it was that Nehekhara became the Land of the Dead.

YEAR 1251: Settra, the king commanded that his mighty war galleys be brought forth from the tomb pits to sail once more upon the river. When this was done according to the king's command, they went forth upon the seas to distant lands in order to seize captives.

YEAR 1252: The return of the war fleet of Khemri bringing captives to be set to work. The king commanded that wells for pure water be sunk and irrigation canals be dug so that Khemri might be restored as in former days. These things were done and the king's heart was gladdened.

YEAR 1520: Prince Dhekhesh went forth against the Khrokodites.

YEAR 1789: The coming of the tomb robbers of the Kazadites to violate and pillage the tombs of kings.

YEAR 2087: Strife in the Necropolis of Numas.

YEAR 2326: The war fleet of the king went forth to seize captives from distant lands on the eleventh occasion of going forth. This time the ships returned empty on account of a battle upon the sea.

YEAR 2588: The coming of sorcerers from among the desert dwellers seeking scrolls. They ransacked the Necropolis of Zandri and slew many Liche Priests who were guarding the scrolls. Then they came unto Khemri and broke into the tombs of kings causing them to awaken in wrath. Great slaughter was made among them.

YEAR 2603: A mighty horde made up of numerous warriors of unknown tribes, clad in iron, came into the land of Nehekhara from the lands of the desert dwellers. They fought against the Tomb Kings of Zandri but turned not into Khemri. Having passed thus across the desert, they disappeared into the wilderness. Some among them despoiled tombs and seized gold and also scrolls of the priests.

YEAR 2877: King Rakaph did battle three times against the desert dwellers and seized tribute.

YEAR 3151: King Settra went forth with his entire army against Numas and overthrew the rebellious ones before they had arisen from their tomb vaults. The stones which had been taken from the Pyramid of the King in former days were brought back into Khemri and the Pyramid of the King was restored.

YEAR 3403: King Qu'a set out from Numas into the high country and seized the places of gold from the Kazadites. Then the Kazadites came down into the Necropolis at Numas to despoil the tombs and fought against the army of five Tomb Kings. Great slaughter was in Numas.

YEAR 3656: The Tilites came into Nehekhara seeking to despoil the Necropolis and carry off gold. They despoiled tombs in the Necropolis of Zandri. King Behedesh and King Memnesh fought against them many times, desisting not in the attack while they remained in the land.

YEAR 3660: Fear all Settra the Imperishable embarks upon his great purge and begins a new age of conquest, seeking to expand his realm. The armies of Nehekhara mass behind him and thus the great expansion begins.

Savage Tribes
Savage Tribes
Expansion of the Legion of Setep
Conquests of Amenemhetum the Great
Conquests of Prince Imrathepis
Tomb of Amenemhetum
The Great Ocean
Silver River
The Plains of Plenty
Nehekharan Patrolled Waters
The Inner Sea
The Sinking Marshes of Khernarch
The Straits of Stars
Zandri
Great Vitae River
The Lush Plains
Lahmia
The Crystal Sea
Bel Aliad
Numas
Khemri
Fertile Lands
Golden River
Heart of Alcadizaar's Empire
Quatar
White Palace
Gateway of Eternity
Valley of the Kings
Mahrak
City of Hope
Lybaras
Gulf of Kharpentharia
The Great Plains
Great Desert of Araby
Bhagar
Rasetra
Ka-Sabar
Elf Ruins
Gulf of Medes
Lizard Pyramid
Jungle
The Jungles of the Gods

The Extent of Alcadizaar the Conqueror's Realm

C-1200 Imperial Calendar

# THE SIEGE OF THE DEAD

The early morning sun sparkled from the tips of twenty thousand spears, glittered across sixty thousand gilded bows and shone radiantly from five thousand chariots. The army of Alcadizaar the Conqueror was spread out across the dunes like a sea of gold and white.

At their back was the massive city wall of Khemri, seventy feet of black granite and green marble rising directly from the sands of the desert, and beyond lay the great city itself picked out in blues, yellows and white. The Black Pyramid loomed over the landscape, casting its great shadow across the lands that had once quailed in fear at the mere mention of a name – Nagash.

Now Alcadizaar stood in defiance of the ancient enemy, his army mustered from the furthest corners of Nehekhara. He had the finest charioteers from his own city of Khemri, deadly archers from Zandri, and the elite Sphinx Legion from Quatar. His right flank was guarded by the Sun Cohort of Prince Imrathepis, guardians of the Gates of Numas. On his left were the chariots of the Jackal Squadron of Mahrak, long time adversaries of the traitorous Lahmians. At the front of Alcadizaar 's army stood trumpeting tuskas, the dark-skinned Ebonian auxiliaries gathered in loose formations around their massive, grey war beasts.

Such a host had not been gathered for many centuries, but now the ancient threat returned. Word came from the east that at the head of the dead army rode Arkhan. – Sorcerer of the Black Tower, thrice-cursed undying general of Nagash. With him came Wsoran, dread blood-drinker of Lahmia who was impervious to mortal weapons and could defeat a hundred men single-handedly. At their back was the army of Lahmia, raised from their graves to march to war once again. If Alcadizaar were to fail in his duty today, all of Nehekhara would be plunged into an era of darkness and death. The vampires would feed upon his loyal subjects, his great palaces would become charnel houses and the long sleep of his ancestors would be defiled by black sorcery.

Alcadizaar watched the rising sun. As he contemplated the battle to come, the distant sky began to darken. A great cloud of blackness seeped over the horizon, leeching all the light and vitality from the air. The sun itself turned dim and soon was lost and the chill of night swept across the desert. He could sense the fear of his soldiers, and heard their disquieted murmurings.

With unnatural speed, the dark storm clouds gathered overhead. In the gloom that was left, the army of the dead advanced. In macabre mockery of the Nehekharan host, chariots of melded bone and sinew raced alongside skeletal cavalry. Archers with their flesh long stripped by carrion advanced with bows bent. Above the sea of bone, ragged banners fluttered in an unearthly breeze and the air itself warped and shifted with magical energy.

Alcadizaar was filled with a deep anger as he watched the shambling horde approach. He thought of the terror that his people had lived under for centuries; the silent threat that had loomed like the shadow of the Black Pyramid over numerous generations of Khemrians. Here and now he would end that threat. He would crush Arkhan's army and cut off the head of Wsoran. He would mount their corpses on the front of his chariot and ride at the head of his host across the mountains to raze the city of Lahmia.

Raising his golden-edged sword into the air, he signalled the advance.

# TALES FROM THE OASIS

Welcome to my humble camp, please be seated and refresh yourself. One of my serving girls will see to all your needs, for here at the Oasis of a Thousand and One Camels all are friends. This paradise of the desert is the last refuge in a god forsaken land, here the living may seek rest, safe in the knowledge that come dawn they will still be breathing. Out there in the great desert of Nehekhara, the dead outnumber the living a thousand to one, and only the brave or the foolish dare trespass on their land – are you brave or foolish my friend? My name is Suli and I am but a humble trader, but my knowledge of these lands is great and perhaps before you venture into the desert of the dead you would take heed of my words.

Countless times have I travelled through the lands of Nehekhara, and yet still each time my belly fills with fear. Just half a day's ride from this very spot lies the ruins of Bel Allad. Once it was a thriving city and the home of my family. That was before the coming of the sleepless ones. As a child I had heard stories of the dead that did not rest. They were as fanciful as the stories of djinns in bottles or of carpets that could sail the skies. Then one accursed summer the breeze that blew the fresh air, cooled by the Great Ocean, suddenly changed direction. For months we were ravaged by an unbearable hot wind that brought with it sandstorms from the east. The fields that surrounded the city failed to produce a harvest and mighty dunes grew around the city walls. Yet even as the people of the city began to perish from starvation and thirst, we still remained hopeful that the storms that burned our throats and flayed our skin would abate.

Then on the eve of the festival of Djaf I witnessed such horror that to this day it still haunts my dreams. Crowds lined the streets in celebration, then without warning the skies grew dark. As if summoned by foul sorceries, a swirling dust storm raced towards the city walls. It reached up to the very heavens themselves, sweeping our cattle into the skies. My people desperately sought shelter, but even as the storm passed our torment was not ended. From the east there came a swarm of insects, the dull hum of their wings growing louder and more intense with each second they drew closer. With savage ferocity they attacked us and I lie to you not, some of these beasts were larger than a man. They burst from the ground itself and the streets became a living carpet of death. They engulfed my people and those who still could fled in fear. Only a handful of us survived and of those few only I, Suli, dares venture back to these lands.

It was a few years later that I returned, a young lad in the employ of my uncle as a camel driver. Our small party had traversed the desert for many days, at times making camp with the nomad tribes who know each and every place to gather water from the accursed dry sands. We had been hired as guides by the manservant of a collector of antiquities for a considerable sum. They wished to make their way to the ancient ruins of the once great city of Khemri. Little could I believe my eyes when I first saw the great pyramids. For many miles a huge black monolith loomed on the horizon dwarfing a second golden pyramid beside it. Even in the harsh glare of the desert sun I felt a coldness surround me as I stared at that dark construct of he who shall not be named. As we drew closer I was astonished to find that the entire city consisted of hundreds, if not thousands, of smaller pyramids. When I say small, please understand, even the most insignificant of these constructions reached a hundred feet into the sky. They littered the desert like a small mountain range and from the top of a dune I could make out a vast labyrinth of alleyways interlacing between the ancient tombs.

We made camp in the old city, insignificant in size compared to the necropolis of the dead. It is the safest place in the region, for they say the dead do not venture within its walls. The stranger who had hired our services left the camp at sunset with just a whip for his protection. A reckless urchin, I could not help but follow him.

He and his servant crossed the dunes and entered the forbidden city. I was eager to follow but my uncle commanded that I stay. Three days passed and we grew weary of waiting. My uncle told me that we would leave come morning and, with this knowledge, that night I crept away from the camp into the necropolis. The tracks of the stranger were easy to follow, for in the city of the dead even the wind is silent. After many hours of weaving in and out of the narrow streets, sometimes following the tracks in circles, I stopped dead in front of a pyramid.

Its entrance lay open but fearful to enter I hid outside, hoping that the stranger would emerge with a hoard of ancient gold and gems. Many hours passed and I fell asleep, dreaming of the wealth I would soon possess. I was woken by a hand on my shoulder; sleepily I opened my eyes, thinking it to be our heroic employer. Instead, before me stood a horror that will be engraved upon my mind to my dying day. A being dressed in ceremonial robes, its brow adorned with a fine gold crown, stood over me. She, and I use the word loosely, was clad in half decayed bandages, and her two lifeless eye sockets stared into my very soul. A bloodied, jewel-studded blade hung at her side. In one hand, bony fingers grasped the severed head of the stranger. I leapt up, my mouth uttering prayers to the gods, and sprinted away, running through dozens of skeletal figures who snatched at my clothes. Arrows fell about me but I was fast and had youth as an ally. Weaving and dodging through the streets, I escaped from the terrible vision.

I do not know how many hours I ran through that vast labyrinth. I can only thank the gods that I found a route out from the necropolis, for there are many who have not been so fortunate. My uncle found me lying face down in the sands. Exhausted and panic stricken I told him of the dead that walked and of the fate of the stranger. We left immediately and to this day my uncle has never returned to the lands of the dead.

After such an encounter, why do I still travel these lands? I ask myself that same question over and over. Whilst awaiting the return of the unfortunate stranger, my head had filled with visions of gold and treasure. From that moment I think my fate was sealed. Riches, my friend, are a strong antidote to fear, and believe me I have seen the riches that these barren lands hide. Many are the expeditions that I guide through these deserts. The seemingly empty lands are filled with an abundance of paradises, buried beneath the deep sands. It is all there for the taking, you just need a good guide and a heart of stone to conquer the fear that will strike through your soul.

Should you wish, for a comparatively small fee I will guide you through the desert. Without my help you will surely not even make it past the Pools of Despair. What foul magics created those mirages I know not, but they have led many to their deaths. As your supplies of water begin to run low suddenly a lush oasis appears before you. Men are driven mad as they strive to reach these false visions. Only four days ago I passed the remains of one such poor individual. His canteen was filled with sand and he had died scooping handfuls of the desert into his mouth, thinking it to be cool water.

I see from your expression that you still doubt your need of my assistance. Even should you make it past the endless mirages and visions, then where would you head? To the north perhaps, where lie the ruins of Zandri. Here the Great Ocean meets the desert and at the mouth of the River Mortis lies this ancient port. Once the great and noble King Amenemhetum ruled over this city. During his reign he built a vast fleet and sailed the oceans, conquering the lands across the seas in the name of Ualatp, the vulture god. His kingdom extended deep into the lands to the north and under his rule Zandri became a fabulous and wealthy place. Now the city is all but destroyed, and the streets are quiet. The seas around Zandri are a different matter though. When the Dark One woke the Tomb Kings they waged war on each other. In death, as he had in life, Amenemhetum was content to be ruler of the oceans. I have seen the King's ships sail the coast with my very own eyes. Ancient vessels, but still as glorious as they were when the King still lived. Even in death it is said he continues to raid the world, his ships ceaselessly sailing the seas, rowed by skeleton slaves doomed to an eternity at the oars. No coast is safe and even the most experienced captains know to steer clear when they sight his fleet. The coast around the Mortis Delta is filled with the sunken wrecks of pirate ships that have foolishly attacked his fleet in search of treasure.

Perhaps you would strike out to the east, for here lies the city of Numas. It is a treacherous route and one which the traveller should tread carefully. You would find yourself passing the Springs of Eternal Life. However, although your canteens would by this time be running low, do not feel tempted to drink of the water. I have witnessed a man do so and, trust me, the immortality he was granted was not one that I envy. No sooner had his lips touched the water than I stood horrified as, before my eyes, his skin withered and he perished in mere seconds. I was rooted to the spot as I watched his skeleton form march into the desert, heedless of my presence. Now I imagine he serves the Tomb Kings, an undying slave at their command.

In Numas they know my name and welcome me, but I am one of a handful of people that is allowed passage through the city gates. In Numas, life has returned to the desert and once again crops grow around the city. Numas is a marvellous place, and over many centuries the pyramids have been restored to their former glory. But do not be fooled into thinking that the people there would welcome you. The Scythans were once a nomad tribe who came to Numas to worship their god. They believe that the Prince of Numas is a manifestation of their god and so have dedicated themselves to his service. Each day they tend to the necropolis, guarding the tombs from those who would seek to defile them. The Prince now rules over the living and the dead and both live in strange harmony. These black-robed nomads patrol the deserts, warning Prince Tutankhanut of any intruders to his realm. In return the nomads are allowed to live in the city under the protection of soldiers who do not sleep. Though why any would feel safety when their lives are guarded by those who are dead is beyond me.

When the Prince goes to war, his chariots race alongside the white Arabian steeds of the Scythan warriors: living and dead fighting side by side. I have heard it said that when a Scythan warrior dies, his body is left in the desert for the carrion to pick his bones clean. After forty days and nights his skeleton is carried back to the tombs where it is prepared so that he may continue to serve the Prince in death as he did when he was alive.

The realm of Nehekhara is indeed massive. Past the mountains lie the cities of Mahrak and Beremas and, of course, the famed temples of Lahmia. It was there that Queen Neferata ruled over the people for centuries. To get to these cities, though, you must first brave the Charnel Valley, also known as the Valley of the Kings, but named by

the nomads the Valley of the Dead. Here at the entrance to the valley lies the magnificent palace of Quatar. Built into the very walls of the canyon pass, it is a truly awesome sight. I have travelled far and wide across this land but never seen such a magnificent piece of architecture. Great pillars carved from the valley rockface line the hundreds of steps that lead to the palace gates. Throughout the entire length of the valley are carved colossal statues, representations of the kings and gods. It is said that a powerful priest has taken residence in the palace and he has learned the secret to bring the statues to life. If you are wise then you would stay clear of that place – no living soul dares travel through the Valley of the Dead, for of the many who have set forth into the valley none have ever returned. Even should you survive, ask yourself what would you seek in Lahmia, for only evil has ever been born in that land of woe.

There is one place that no amount of money could tempt me to take you to. Be wary of marching to the south for there an evil exudes across the desert sands. It is here that Arkhan the Black built his tower. Arkhan who fought at the side of He Who Shall Not Be Named. Arkhan, who slew countless tribes and even gave his own life to protect the greatest evil that has ever set foot in this land. After his death, the tower lay dormant; a shattered, empty husk that even the scorpions avoided.

Recently I have word from the nomad tribes to the south that the tower is inhabited once again. No one can be certain who lives in the tower now, as each dawn, when the sun's rays cross the dunes, the tower vanishes from where it stands to appear in some other location in the desert. The nomads say that Arkhan has risen and once more seeks to cast his shadow across the land. This is grave news for all, for if Arkhan the Black has returned then all should fear lest his master soon follow. If this is true then all in this land should take heed. The Tomb Kings whom we fear so greatly could soon prove to be our only salvation.

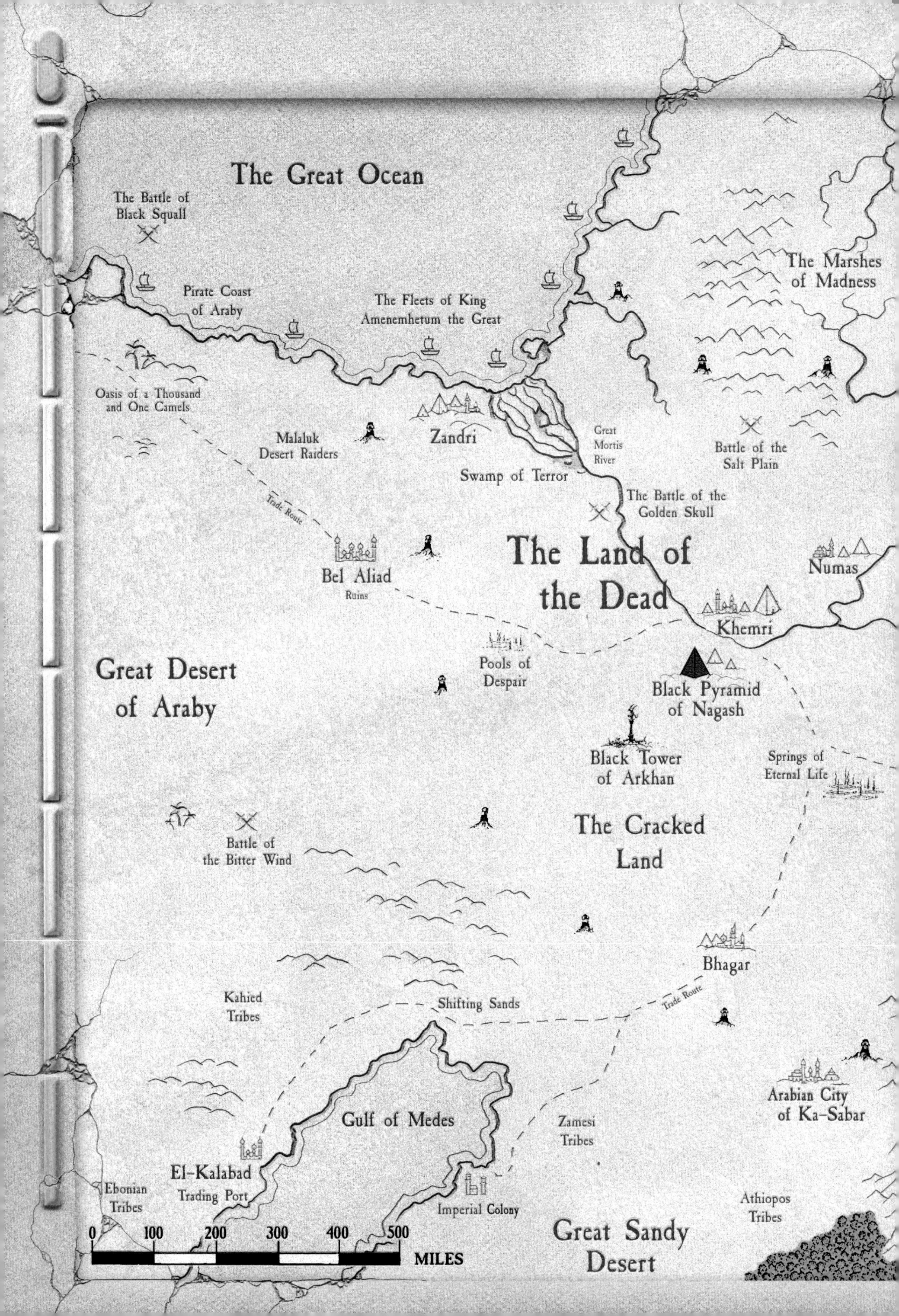

The Great Ocean
The Battle of Black Squall
Pirate Coast of Araby
The Fleets of King Amenemhetum the Great
The Marshes of Madness
Oasis of a Thousand and One Camels
Malaluk Desert Raiders
Zandri
Great Mortis River
Swamp of Terror
Battle of the Salt Plain
The Battle of the Golden Skull
Trade Route
Bel Aliad
Ruins
The Land of the Dead
Numas
Khemri
Pools of Despair
Great Desert of Araby
Black Pyramid of Nagash
Black Tower of Arkhan
Springs of Eternal Life
The Cracked Land
Battle of the Bitter Wind
Bhagar
Kahied Tribes
Shifting Sands
Trade Route
Arabian City of Ka-Sabar
Gulf of Medes
Zamesi Tribes
El-Kalabad Trading Port
Ebonian Tribes
Imperial Colony
Athiopos Tribes
Great Sandy Desert
0 100 200 300 400 500
MILES

The Plain of Bones
Desolation of Nagash
The Sour Sea
Nagashizzar
Below which lies the Cursed Pit
Battle of the Grey Hag
The Fortress of Vorag
Ruins
Misty Mountain
The Broken Teeth
Blight Water
The Straits of Nagash
Red Cloud Mountain
Mortis Tarn
Cursed Lahmia
Doom Mountain
The Bitter Sea
The Battle of Phar's Legion
Ash River
Devil's Backbone
Battle of
ne Mighty Flame
Gulf of Fear
Lybaras
Mahrak
City of Decay
Resting Place of Queen Khalida
Quatar
Palace of Corpses
Charnal Valley
Doom Glade Swamp
The Cursed Jungle
Battle of the Old Gods
Mount Arachnos
Crater of the Walking Dead
Temple of Skulls
Lost Plateau
Rasetra
Lost Hold
ak Zorn
KEY TO MAP OF THE LAND OF THE DEAD
Settlement
Battle
Necropolis
Oasis
Fleet
Jungle
Trade Route
Volcano
Tower Delineating Borders of Nehekhara

The clatter of metal crashing on stone echoed through the corridors of the ancient dust-filled tomb. Inside an ornate gold sarcophagus, the entombed king opened his shrivelled eyelids, revealing two black, empty soulless sockets.

"Leave it Gribbit, that stuff ain't worth nuffin'," a high pitched, raspy voice called out to its comrade.

"Shut it Ragwort, da boss likes big swords and dis one is dead shiny," a second voice called back.

Gribbit stepped over the huge pile of fallen spears and shields carrying a curved golden blade that was as long as he was tall. He scurried up to his Goblin colleague who was rooting around in a chest full of jewellery and gems. Ragwort was already throwing the valuable necklaces around his neck and only stopped when he felt his knees buckle with the weight.

The small dark chamber was suddenly illuminated as the torches on the walls flared into light. Both of the Goblins froze, staring at each other, eyes wide in fear. Burdened by their ill-gotten treasures, neither Goblin was able to flee fast enough to escape the sword, as it swept down in an arc severing the heads of the two thieves with one fell swipe.

The bandage-clad figure left the ransacked chamber, walking down corridors that had not been disturbed for centuries. Reaching what appeared to be a blocked passageway he laid a bony hand on the wall, pressing his long white digits into a recess on the surface. Stone grated heavily on stone as a doorway framed by light appeared before him, the bright glare of the desert sun banishing the darkness of the corridor.

From his elevated position high on the pyramid, the Tomb King watched the dust cloud of an army marching to the north, away from his necropolis. The smaller pyramids lay broken and the once proud colonnade of statues that led to the necropolis had now been unceremoniously toppled. The Undead king watched as a lone figure climbed up the steep steps to where he stood. As the ancient human, dressed in fine ceremonial robes reached the top, he rested his weight on his staff in an attempt to catch his breath. The Tomb King turned to face his servant, addressing him in an ancient tongue.

"Priest, summon my army."

* * *

King Phar stood unmoving upon his ornate war chariot. In the distance the Tomb King heard the deep, heavy pounding of tribal drums alerting the Orcs to his army's approach. He had experienced that same sound many centuries ago when blood flowed within his mortal flesh. Back then, those same drumbeats had chilled his blood with the thought of the coming battle. Now he felt nothing but cold contempt for these pitiful creatures. In over two thousand years they had not developed as a civilisation and he would be glad to purge them from the face of the world. The greenskins poured out from the camp's crude wooden gate. At first they seemed an undisciplined shambling horde, but the Tomb King knew better than to underestimate their instinctive warlike abilities. Within minutes a solid wall of greenskins faced his army and advanced forwards. Guttural chants sounded out over the pounding of the drums as the Orcs went to war.

From Phar's commanding viewpoint, the neat and disciplined ranks of his own army were dwarfed by the advancing, teeming horde.

"Your majesty." King Phar turned to face the Liche Priest who addressed him. "What is your will?"

The king turned his crowned skeletal head towards his archers. He raised his sword and with that signal the skeleton archers loosed their arrows skyward. Before the first cloud of arrows had descended into the Orc ranks, a second volley was airborne. King Phar watched with satisfaction as arrows that appeared to be sailing over the heads of the enemy twisted in mid-flight, careering down into the centre of the Orcs' formations. Dozens fell with the first volley, followed by more seconds later. Within minutes, the once solid wall of Orcs was in disarray as the onslaught of enchanted missiles continued to fall. Orcs began to flee back towards their camp and within the first few minutes of battle it appeared as though the Orc army had been defeated.

Then from the Orc camp came the heavy pounding of hooves on soil. Bursting from the gates rode a mighty Orc. Mounted on a huge boar and clad in an assortment of thick plate armour, he bawled at the panic stricken Orcs, who now turned once more to face the King's army. Undaunted by the hail of arrows that rained down amongst their ranks, the Orcs again marched forward, quickening their pace as they closed in on Phar's loyal soldiers. The King signalled to his troops again and the skeleton archer formations closed their ranks, forming into defensive blocks. Gaps in the solid line had now been opened and the rumble of wheels and clatter of skeletal hooves sounded across the battlefield as the King's cavalry and chariots rode forwards. Suddenly, a dark shadow sped across the ground, growing larger by the second. Phar looked up to see a huge bat-like creature sailing down towards the newly reformed skeletons. With a mighty crash, bone splintered and broke as the creature descended into the midst of his force. He spied a second shadow and this time could make out the form of a winged Goblin diving to his doom. This time the suicidal creature crashed behind the formation, leaving a bloody pulp of metal, flesh and canvas on the dusty ground. Phar spotted a small line of Goblins behind the Orc lines, flapping huge canvas wings in anticipation of launching themselves skywards from a huge catapult contraption. Uttering an ancient incantation, Phar was more than satisfied to see the ground around the catapult crack and split as a huge scorpion rose from out of the earth. Its massive pincers sliced one of the machine's crew in half before its immense stinger thrust forwards, repeatedly striking the small Goblins who fell to the floor, convulsing as the poison took hold. The sudden attack terrified the doom divers who ran in panic, flapping furiously in a vain attempt to get airborne and out of reach of the monstrous beast.

By now the Orcs were so close to the front line that King Phar could see the grizzly trophies that hung round their necks. Amongst the teeth and skulls that adorned their necks was the odd gold neckpiece, ancient treasures from Phar's own collection. Calmly, the King reached out and grasped a huge flail from a weapon rack on the front of the chariot. It had been a long time since Phar had used this weapon and its weight felt good in his hands. The weapon's ornate carved handle ended with a series of chains, from which hung the skulls of conquered enemies. For a brief moment the skulls crackled with small flashes of lightning. Spurring his steeds into action, Phar's chariot rolled slowly forwards, gradually picking up speed.

Following his lead, the rest of the army marched as one towards the Orcs. The King signalled to the chariot next to him. A gold armoured icon bearer nodded in acknowledgement and waved his long staff, topped with a crescent and engraved down the length with hieroglyphs that told of the bearer's heroic feats. In life, the icon bearer had been Phar's mightiest champion and the King's own personal bodyguard, now in death he still rode to war at his King's side. The dusty ground to the Orcs' right flank cracked and split apart as a dozen skeletal steeds rode from the ground itself. They charged into the surprised Orcs' flank and with this shock attack, the King signalled for the rest of the army's chariots and cavalry to charge. The decorated constructions smashed into the ranks of the greenskins, gold trimmed wheels crushing the Orcs beneath them. Orcs fled before the combined onslaught and spears thrust through their unprotected backs. Phar's chariot rolled over several bodies before smashing into the boar riders, who had been taken by surprise by the severity of the charge. Phar spotted the Orc warboss, and steering the steeds towards the massive foe, he swung his flail in a wide arc above his head. The warboss leapt off his boar to avoid the collision. A crunch of wood followed as the chariot splintered at the impact with the huge beast.

Within seconds the Orc was on his feet and swinging his massive crude choppa at Phar's head. The Orc's blow fell wide and the King brought his flail down in a powerful sweep. With a sickening crunch the skulls smashed into the Orc before he could strike, shattering even his thick-boned head. Seeing their warboss fall was more than the greenskins could take, and as their courage failed them the cowardly savages fled to the safety of the mountains.

As his warriors picked the jewellery off the corpses and carried it back to the Liche Priest, King Phar surveyed the land around him. During his reign he had cleared much of this mountainous region of Orc tribes. Soon the time would come when he would conquer these lands again, but for now he was satisfied that the Orcs would think long and hard before disturbing his sleep once more.

Back in the ruins of Mahrak, the torches in the small tomb chamber slowly burned out and the recovered treasures in the alcoves of the pyramid vanished in the darkness. Encased in his sarcophagus, King Phar once again closed his eyes, his arms crossed upon his chest, and grasped in one hand was the flail, now adorned with a new skull with huge fang-like teeth.

# LEGIONS OF THE TOMB KINGS

*This section of the book is the Bestiary. In it we will be looking at the different troop types, heroes, monsters and war engines of the Tomb Kings armies.*

## UNDEAD

All models listed in the Tomb Kings army list are Undead.

Note that the Undead special rules for Tomb Kings armies are slightly different from those for Vampire Counts armies due to the differences in the magic animating them.

All Undead in the Tomb Kings army list have the following special rules:

### The General

The army must include at least one Tomb King or Tomb Prince, who will be the army's General. If the army includes more than one Tomb King or Prince, the one with the highest Leadership will be the General. In the case of two or more characters having the same Leadership value, the player can decide which will be the General. Remember to tell your opponent which model is the General at the beginning of the battle.

### The Hierophant

The army must include at least one Liche Priest or High Priest who will be the army's Hierophant, the one responsible for the awakening of the entire army from their ancient slumber.

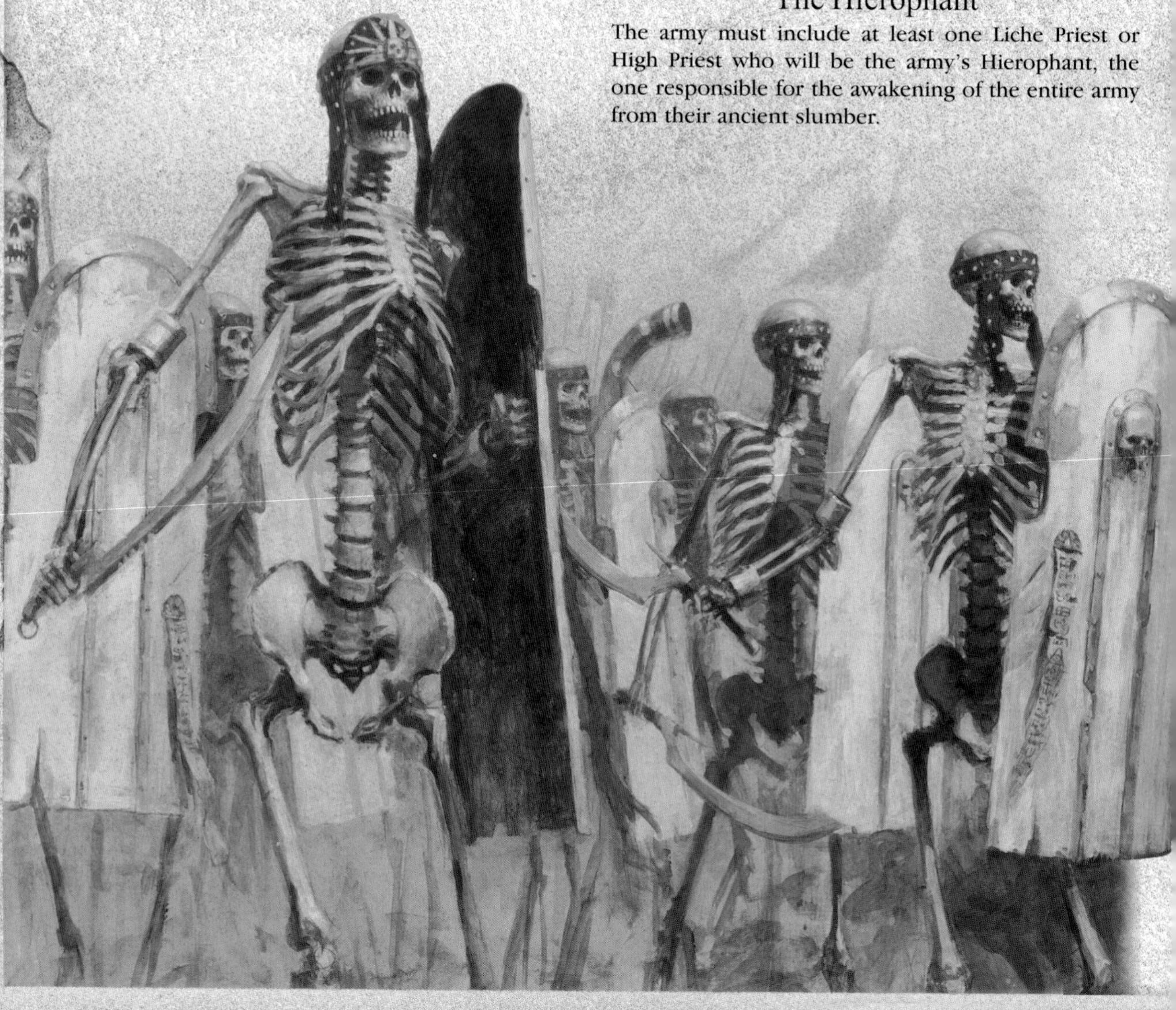

If the army includes more than one Liche Priest or High Priest, the one with the highest Leadership will be the Hierophant. In the case of two or more characters having the same Leadership, the player can decide which is the Hierophant. Remember to tell your opponent which model is the Hierophant at the beginning of the battle.

If the Hierophant is destroyed, the Undead in the army will start to slowly crumble to dust. To represent this, at the end of the phase when the Hierophant is killed, and at the beginning of every Undead turn thereafter, all Undead units on the battlefield must take a Leadership test. If the test is failed, the unit suffers a number of wounds equal to the number they failed the Leadership test by. No saves of any kind (not even Ward saves or Regeneration) are allowed against such wounds. Eg, a unit of Skeletons (Ld 3) takes the test and rolls a 7 – the unit suffers 4 wounds (7-3=4). Characters never suffer wounds because of a destroyed Hierophant. Units can use the Leadership of a character leading the unit for this test or the General's Leadership if he's within 12", as normal. If a character is riding in a chariot and he is not with a unit of chariots, his chariot has to take this test but it can use the character's Leadership value. The Hierophant has to be destroyed (ie, permanently removed from the table) for this rule to take effect.

## Break Tests

Undead cannot be broken, but Undead units beaten in combat suffer one additional wound for every point they lose the combat by (no saves of any kind, not even Regeneration or Ward saves, are allowed against such wounds). If characters are present in the unit, or if they are riding in a chariot, the controlling player can decide how to allocate the wounds among the unit, the chariot and the characters. In multiple combats, each Undead unit on the losing side suffers one additional wound for every point their side has lost the combat by. If an Undead unit is wiped out by combat resolution in the first turn of a combat, the enemy gets the option to make an overrun move as normal.

## Arrows of the Asp

The ranks of the Tomb Kings army advance relentlessly towards the foe, able to fire on the move without loss of accuracy. Their arrows are blessed by the Asp Goddess and seek out their enemies unerringly. Undead models in a Tomb Kings army do not count any penalties or bonuses to hit when shooting.

## Battle Standard

Undead that are within 12" of their Battle Standard suffer one less wound than they normally would when defeated in combat. Eg, a unit of Skeletons loses a combat by 3. They should lose three extra Skeletons but, because the Battle Standard is within 12", they only lose two models.

## Immune To Psychology

Undead are Immune to Psychology (see page 112 of the Warhammer rulebook).

## Cause Fear

Undead cause *fear* (Warhammer rulebook, page 81).

## Marching

Undead cannot make a march move.

## Charge Reactions

Undead can only react to charges by holding.

# TOMB KINGS

"Lord of the Earth, Lord of the Sky, Ruler of the Four Horizons, Mighty Lion of the Infinite Desert, Great Hawk of the Heavens, Radiant Sun, King of the Shifting Sands, Reigning Till the End of Time, Eternal Sovereign, Vanquisher of Enemies, He who Holds the Sceptre, Khemrikhara, Settra the Imperishable!"

A selection of the names and titles of Settra, greatest Tomb King of Khemri

Tomb Kings are the ancient and long-dead rulers of the land of Nehekhara. There have been countless kings during the long history of that ancient land. Each city was ruled by a separate dynasty and these were ousted from power and replaced by others over the span of centuries. The Tomb Kings regularly waged war upon each other to spread their influence over the entire land of Nehekhara. Greatest of all the kings were those of Khemri, which was the largest and most proud of the ancient cities. It became established early on that whoever ruled in Khemri was the mightiest king in Nehekhara, to whom the other kings would pledge allegiance and offer tribute. All the kings shared the same lust for worldly wealth and power, and the same ambition to defy death. To this end they founded the Mortuary Cult in order to reawaken them after death. They directed the building of great pyramids surrounded by extensive necropoli as strongholds for all eternity, and ordered that they be mummified and entombed within to preserve their physical bodies for all time.

The Tomb Kings are mummified corpses awakened and inhabited by their undying spirits. Their skeletal bodies are dried husks, preserved with pitch and wrapped in bandages inscribed with magical incantations. Bedecked in gleaming crowns and the regalia of kingship, they retain all the majesty that they exuded while alive. Amulets and talismans of gold inset with precious stones hang around their necks, and they often wear the breastplate of a military commander strapped over their death-shroud wrappings. Entombed within the same deep chamber is their kingly chariot and steeds, ready for them to ride forth from the tomb shaft into the light of day. Revived by the rituals of their priests, the Tomb Kings awake from their death-sleep possessing all the ambition and craving for power that they had in life and are bent on restoring their ancient realms. If this means the reconquest of former wide dominions then this shall be done, for a Tomb King's army, loyal even in death, rises from its rest at his call and is ready to march at his side once again.

Tomb Princes are the sons of the Tomb Kings. Each of the kings of ancient Nehekhara kept extensive harems and so had many sons. Only one of these princes of the blood could succeed his father to the throne. As for the others, some died heroically in battle, and their bodies were brought home to be mummified and entombed in a place within the king's pyramid, as befitted captains of high rank. There they await in the sleep of death, ready to recommence their military duties at the time of their awakening. Others lived on to serve their brother as officers and were thus entombed in his pyramid to continue to serve him after death. The Tomb Princes rest in their vaults beside the great tomb chamber of their sovereign in an eternal council of war, waiting for the moment of awakening when they shall resume command of their contingents. Those few who, through jealousy or intrigue, attempted to usurp the throne were denied the privilege of mummification and their bones were thrown to the carrion of the desert.

| | M | WS | BS | S | T | W | I | A | Ld |
|---|---|---|---|---|---|---|---|---|---|
| Tomb King | 4 | 6 | 4 | 5 | 5 | 4 | 3 | 4 | 10 |
| Tomb Prince | 4 | 5 | 4 | 4 | 5 | 3 | 3 | 3 | 9 |

## SPECIAL RULES

**Flammable**

Tomb Kings and Tomb Princes have had their ancient bodies preserved through elaborate embalming ceremonies performed by their priests, and are wrapped in pitch-soaked bandages. Tomb Kings and Tomb Princes are Flammable (see p.114 of the Warhammer rulebook).

**The Curse**

A powerful curse hangs over the mummified corpses of the royalty of Nehekhara, striking down those who seek to do them wrong. Countless tales abound of tomb robbers aging a lifetime in mere seconds, and songs lament those who would dare strike down these ancient warriors! The model responsible for the destruction of a Tomb King or Tomb Prince (ie, the model that causes the final wound) must immediately take a Leadership test. If the test is failed, the model will suffer D6 wounds that cannot be saved in any way (including Ward saves) nor Regenerated. If no single model can be identified as responsible for the Tomb King/Prince's destruction (eg, he is destroyed by missile fire from an entire unit), the unit responsible must pass a Leadership test or suffer D6 wounds randomised as missile hits. If the Tomb King/Prince was slain by a model riding a monster, randomise hits between the rider and his mount.

If more than one unit is responsible for causing the last wound on a Tomb King/Prince at the same time (eg, he is destroyed by combat resolution in a multiple combat), then all guilty units must take the test as above!

**"My Will be done!"**
Although it is the magic of the Liche Priests that animates the Tomb King's army, it is also by the will and force of personality of the Tomb King himself that they move and fight. Tomb Kings and Princes are powerful leaders, able to instil their warriors with their own vigour.

A Tomb King may cast two Incantations (either Mankara's Incantation of Urgency or Horekhah's Incantation of Righteous Smiting) at a Power Level of D6, using them either on himself and a unit he has joined or on any other friendly Tomb Kings unit within 6". He may cast the same Incantation twice.

A Tomb Prince may cast Mankara's Incantation of Urgency or Horekhah's Incantation of Righteous Smiting during the Magic phase on himself, or himself and the unit he has joined if he is with a unit. This Incantation is cast at a Power Level of D6.

# LICHE PRIESTS

"Revered One, Venerable One, Lord of Secrets, High Priest of the Temple of Years, Keeper of the Pyramid of Eternity, Interpreter of Mysteries, Prophet of the Lord of the Tomb, Master of Awakenings, Bearer of the Serpent Staff, Khatep, the Enduring."

Names and titles of Khatep, Liche High Priest of Khemri.

In their desire to defy death, the kings of Nehekhara founded the Mortuary Cult and appointed the priesthood, of which the Liche Priests are all that remain. The priests were commanded to study the arts of mummification and communion with the gods. Steadily, over many centuries, the priests learned how to preserve a corpse from decay until the art of mummification had become very elaborate. They also devised a vast lore of incantations and rituals intended to enable the dead king, as well as his entire court and army, to be awakened from death. The first generations of priests, whose skills and knowledge were rudimentary, died after prolonging their own lives far beyond their natural span. They passed on their knowledge to the next generation of priests who exceeded them in wisdom and expertise. In this way, their knowledge accumulated until the fifth generation of priests who did not die, though their bodies slowly withered away until they were little more than living corpses. Thus the entire priesthood became the Liche Priests, able to officiate the Mortuary Cult of their king in perpetuity, and they held great power in the land. Indeed, they were the only subjects of the king who could not be executed, since he depended on their knowledge and loyalty in order to live beyond his own death. In this way the priesthood became a formidable power behind the throne.

Each necropolis, with the pyramid of the Tomb King at its core, has a temple dedicated to the king's Mortuary Cult. Here resides the Liche High Priests served by many lesser priests. Only the High Priests have been initiated into the deepest secrets of the cult. The priests have many duties to perform in the necropolis apart from the Ritual of Awakening, including such tasks as renewing the seals upon the portals of the tomb vaults, remaking inscriptions which have become eroded by wind blown sand, determining the moment of awakening and consulting the spirit of the Tomb King by means of oracles. They continue to perform these duties for centuries because they cannot die a natural death. Little more than long decayed corpses, their dry, wizened skin, resembling that of a mummy, is stretched like old parchment over their brittle skeleton.

| | M | WS | BS | S | T | W | I | A | Ld |
|---|---|---|---|---|---|---|---|---|---|
| Liche High Priest | 4 | 3 | 3 | 3 | 3 | 3 | 2 | 1 | 9 |
| Liche Priest | 4 | 3 | 3 | 3 | 3 | 2 | 2 | 1 | 8 |

## SPECIAL RULES

**Liche Priests**
Liche Priests and their magic are discussed in full in the Tomb Kings Magic section starting on page 34.

# SKELETON SOLDIERS

"The mighty army of the Necropolis, awaiting the command of their lord. Valiant soldiers all, who rise up at the call of their lord and master."

Hieroglyphic inscription over the tomb pits
of the Skeleton Legions of Settra.

The mighty armies of the Tomb Kings, made up of regiment after regiment of valiant soldiers, swore an oath of loyalty before the gods to serve the king beyond death. Thus the bones of those soldiers who perished in battle were collected from the field of war and interred in the great tomb pits of the king's necropolis.

Those who yet lived after their lord had died marched as if on a victory parade to the necropolis upon the day of the king's entombment. Here they stood in their regiments, ready for death. Arranged before the pyramid of their king in ranks, icons held proudly, they were entombed alive. No soldier flinched as the great stones were heaved into position blocking out the light of the sun. Bravely they stood to attention as the sand was poured into the tomb pits until the tops of their standard poles disappeared from sight. There they remain until the trumpet call of the Liche Priests awakens them and they once again heed the orders of their commanders.

These skeletal soldiers fight in the same manner that they did when living. Highly disciplined in life, the foot soldiers of the Tomb Kings fight in highly organised ranks, turning and advancing in perfect unison. Archers unleash their arrows in great clouds that darken the sky, blessed by the Asp Goddess so that they seek out their foes with unerring accuracy. Mounted on the skeletal remains of their once proud steeds, regiments of cavalry race across the open plains to engage their foes, while other, more lightly armoured horsemen scout out the movements of the enemy, and harrass their flanks.

These soldiers of the Tomb Kings, loyal for all eternity, continue to practise their ways of war as they did in centuries long past.

| | M | WS | BS | S | T | W | I | A | Ld |
|---|---|---|---|---|---|---|---|---|---|
| Skeleton | 4 | 2 | 2 | 3 | 3 | 1 | 2 | 1 | 3 |
| Skel. Horseman | 4 | 2 | 2 | 3 | 3 | 1 | 2 | 1 | 5 |
| Skeletal Steed | 8 | 2 | 0 | 3 | 3 | 1 | 2 | 1 | 5 |

## SPECIAL RULES

**Fast Cavalry**

Skeleton Light Horsemen are classed as fast cavalry (see page 117 of the Warhammer rulebook).

# SKELETON CHARIOTS

"The swift charioteers of the king. They who pursue the foes of the sovereign on the day of his awakening."

Hieroglyphic inscription over the tomb pits of the Skeleton Charioteers of Settra.

The pride of a Tomb King's army are his charioteers. Nehekhara was the first great civilisation of Mankind, and the place where Men first used horse and chariot in battle. The ancient armies of Nehekhara included strong forces of swift, lightly built chariots usually drawn by a pair of horses. These fought in massed units and were considered the elite of the army, and only the nobility were permitted to fight as charioteers. This was considered a great accomplishment, for in ancient Nehekhara horses had only recently been bred as beasts of war.

These elite chariot squadrons were entombed beside the pyramids of the Tomb Kings of Nehekhara, ready to serve their lords upon their awakening, and trample over their foes as they had done in his mortal reign. Admired and respected foes when they were alive, the skeletal charioteers of the Tomb Kings riding to battle strike fear in the hearts of all who oppose them.

| | M | WS | BS | S | T | W | I | A | Ld |
|---|---|---|---|---|---|---|---|---|---|
| Chariot | – | – | – | 4 | 4 | 3 | – | – | – |
| Skeleton | – | 3 | 2 | 3 | – | – | 2 | 1 | 7 |
| Skel. Champion | – | 3 | 2 | 3 | – | – | 2 | 2 | 7 |
| Skeletal Steed | 8 | 2 | – | 3 | – | – | 2 | 1 | – |

## SPECIAL RULES

**Light Chariots**

Nehekharan light chariots follow the rules for chariots on page 126-128 of the Warhammer rulebook with the following exceptions:

Light chariots can be formed up into units of chariots (see page 127 of the Warhammer rulebook). These units also follow the rules for fast cavalry (see page 117 of the Warhammer rulebook).

Light chariots cause D3 impact hits instead of D6.

Light chariots have a Unit Strength of 3 per model (4 if ridden by a character).

Light chariots offer less protection to characters riding in them. When shooting against a character riding in a light chariot, attacks will hit the character on a 5+ instead of a 6, and a light chariot confers to the character a +1 Armour save instead of the normal +2 save.

## Chariot Units

*As Tomb Kings armies can make wide use of chariot units, here is a summary and some clarifications of the chariot unit rules:*

- *Chariots rank up just like infantry and cavalry models, and benefit fully from any command models they may have.*
- *A character model inside a unit of chariots will only benefit from the "Look Out, Sir!" rule if the unit includes five or more rank and file chariots.*
- *Wounds on a Chariot unit Champion do not carry over into the rank and file, and vice versa. In other words, the rank and file lose a chariot for every 3 wounds suffered, and the unit Champion is destroyed once he has suffered 3 wounds.*
- *Chariots can only be joined by characters also on chariots, and characters on chariots may only join chariot units. This means that if the character is with a unit when his chariot is destroyed, from the end of the phase he is no longer part of the unit (you might like to place him 1" away to make sure this is clear).*
- *If a chariot is wounded in close combat by a weapon that has Strength 7 or higher it is automatically destroyed. In this case, all the wounds that the chariot had remaining are counted towards combat resolution.*

# TOMB GUARD

"Sentinels at the portal of Eternity, Mighty ones who stand before the King, Valiant ones whom none shall pass, Guardians of the King's Tomb."

Hieroglyphic inscription over the tomb pit of the Tomb Guards of Settra.

The bravest and best soldiers serving the Tomb King acted as his personal bodyguards and palace guards during their lifetime. In respect of this role, they were honoured with the privilege of sharing his immortality and buried close to their king within the regal pyramid itself. Just as they guarded the palace in life, so now they guard the inner sanctum of the necropolis. The prospect of sharing in the immortality of their king and serving him for all time inspired these soldiers to heroic acts of bravery. They would die where they stood rather than retreat, and would charge against the most hopeless odds. Time and again this would bring victory to the king's army and earn a place in his pyramid for the fallen. Tomb Guard were also honoured with partial mummification, though this was nowhere near as elaborate as the ceremonies of preparation which the Tomb Kings and Princes underwent.

The Tomb Guard were entombed with the finest armour and weapons, as well as gold decorations proclaiming their bravery and devotion. They rest in their sarcophagi, standing upright around the royal tomb chamber. Here they stand to attention as palace guards until the time comes when they are again needed. If intruders violate the tomb, they will awaken and defend their lord. If the king awakens ready to go forth to conquer and trample the lands of the living beneath his chariot, they arise and form up at his side.

Just as the Tomb Guard were once the elite warriors of the Tomb King, the Icon Bearer was his trusted champion. Only the greatest and most trusted of warriors was given the honour of carrying the king's personal icon to battle. The Icon Bearer was also the envoy and herald of the Tomb King, given the duty of bearing his lord's commands to distant parts of the realm and dispense justice in the king's name. Often disputes between Tomb Kings of different cities would be settled by a ritual duel between their nominated champions, and the Icon Bearer often fulfilled this role.

| | M | WS | BS | S | T | W | I | A | Ld |
|---|---|---|---|---|---|---|---|---|---|
| Icon Bearer | 4 | 4 | 3 | 4 | 4 | 2 | 3 | 2 | 8 |
| Tomb Guard | 4 | 3 | 3 | 4 | 4 | 1 | 3 | 1 | 8 |
| Champion | 4 | 3 | 3 | 4 | 4 | 1 | 3 | 2 | 8 |

## SPECIAL RULES

**Tomb Blades**
Tomb Guard were excellent soldiers during their lives and gifted with powerful weapons that had incantations of cursing imbued into them. Any normal weapon carried by a Tomb Guard or Icon Bearer counts as a magic weapon (but all the normal rules for that weapon still apply). The weapon also has the Killing Blow special rule (see page 112 of the Warhammer rulebook). Note that this rule does not apply to any magic weapon that an Icon Bearer takes from the magic items list.

# USHABTI

"They stand staring into the sun for eternity, the physical embodiments of the everlasting gods. Tremble ye who look upon their divine forms!"

Inscription at the base of the Ushabti depicting the great gods of Nehekhara, at the entrance to the Great Pyramid of Rakaph I.

Carved into the likeness of the many gods and goddesses of Nehekhara, the Ushabti stand as guardian statues around the perimeter of the great pyramids of the Tomb Kings. Standing three times the height of a man, they are imposing monuments, and all who pass beneath their shadows tremble. In times of need, the Liche Priests imbue the Ushabti with tremendous power through complex incantations and charms. As the chants are completed, the Ushabti step from their plinths and daises, silent and ready to be directed to war. In ancient times, the warriors of Nehekhara took great strength from the fact that the Ushabti fought with them, for who could not be inspired by the physical representations of the gods marching into battle by their sides!

| | M | WS | BS | S | T | W | I | A | Ld |
|---|---|---|---|---|---|---|---|---|---|
| Ushabti | 5 | 4 | 0 | 6 | 4 | 3 | 3 | 3 | 10 |

## SPECIAL RULES

**Undead Constructs**
Ushabti are not reanimated skeletons like the bulk of a Tomb King's army but bound by powerful magic placed inside their inanimate shells. As a result, they are more resilient than normal Undead and always count as if they are within 12" of the Battle Standard, even if there is no Battle Standard on the table. If they actually are within 12" of the Battle Standard then they will benefit from that as well, losing two less Wounds than they should from lost combats. In addition, Undead Constructs have a 5+ Armour save.

It was the Nehekharans' belief that their gods dwelt in the Great Land in the time before the birth of Man. It is said that the span of the deities' lives was numbered in millions of years. After this golden era when the gods walked as men, they became invisible spirits, able to take on any form that they desired. Thus it was that Asaph, goddess of beauty, magic and vengeance, chose the form of the asp, and Khsar took on the elemental form of the desert wind.

Most depictions of the gods in this grand pantheon show them in these powerful forms, and they are commonly carved as guardian Ushabti in the tombs of kings. Some of the most common statues include Djaf, the swift to anger jackal-headed god, and Phakth the deity of the hawk, who is said to be able to see the evil and sins of the dead. Ptra, the Sun God, was the most widely worshipped of all the numerous divinities, symbolising eternity and immortality. In the stories recorded in numerous inscriptions, Ptra is said to ride his golden chariot across the skies, forever chasing his beloved, the moon-goddess.

The Gods Qu'aph, Ualatp and Sokth took the form of the cobra, vulture and scorpion, while others chose the crocodile, the ibis or particular stone formations of the desert. Some divinities took no particular form, and it is these that are the most mysterious and sinister of all. Pha'a and Usekhp are two of these gods, said to dwell in spirit form within almighty tombs buried beneath the sands, and their names are used in the direst of curses and invocations.

# TOMB SWARMS

"Behold! The dead, stinging ones shall come forth from their abodes beneath the sands. Their numbers shall be beyond counting..."

Part of an incantation used by the High Priest Karrahtut to summon a voracious swarm to consume his enemies, recounted in hieroglyphs in the great Necropolis of Bahgar.

The tombs of the necropoli are infested with the dried husks and shells of countless poisonous insects and other vicious creatures of the desert. Though long dead, the mere presence of the Liche Priests and Tomb Kings fills their empty shells with animation, and they scuttle from their hiding places around the mortuary temples and beneath the sands. The Liche Priests have long since gained mastery over these creatures and can summon them forth at will through their incantations. They do this to guard the necropolis against intruders, especially tomb robbers. Those who penetrate the labyrinthine passages of the tombs risk these swarms appearing seemingly from the earth itself in an unstoppable wave, biting, clawing and burying themselves in flesh. The victims are poisoned by hundreds of bites and stings, and are rapidly devoured as the vicious creatures quickly consume flesh, clothing and bone.

| | M | WS | BS | S | T | W | I | A | Ld |
|---|---|---|---|---|---|---|---|---|---|
| Tomb Swarm | 4 | 3 | 0 | 2 | 2 | 5 | 1 | 5 | 10 |

## SPECIAL RULES

**Swarm**
Tomb Swarms represent countless numbers of creatures on a single 40mm x 40mm base. This base is treated as a single model with several Wounds and Attacks. A Tomb Swarm base fights at full effect until it has taken 5 Wounds at which point it is removed. Tomb Swarms are Unbreakable and cannot be joined by characters.

**Small**
Tomb Swarms don't block the line of sight of other units. Note that this does not, however, allow other skirmishers to move through their formation.

**Skirmishers**
A unit of Tomb Swarm bases follows the skirmishers rules.

**Poisoned Attacks**
Tomb Swarms have Poisoned Attacks.

**"It Came From Below..."**
Tomb Swarms do not have to be deployed at the beginning of the game, and can use the "It Came From Below..." rules given opposite if they choose.

# TOMB SCORPION

"Fear them – guardians of the Underworld who stalk among us!"

Part of a hieroglyphic inscription carved into one of the great Tomb Scorpions of Numas.

Tomb Scorpions are powerful creations of the Liche Priests, giant constructs carved and moulded into representations of the giant, mystical creatures said to guard the entrance to the Nehekharan underworld. They are formed from a combination of materials: stone, wood and metal, together with the bones and shells of long dead mighty creatures that are scattered beneath the sands of the desert. Through laborious and precise incantations, the Liche Priests join the materials into a single form. The Tomb Scorpion serves as a sarcophagus or tomb itself, for the shell of the construct is formed around the cadaverous body of one of the ancient High Priests. For reasons unknown, some of these ancient ones no longer respond to the Incantations of Awakening and have fallen into what is known as the Death Sleep.

That these beings are truly dead is doubtful, as their power can still be felt exuding from their skeletal bodies.

The shell of the inanimate scorpion is inscribed with hieroglyphs of binding, and a ceremony of awakening is spoken. This ceremony lasts from moonrise until the first rays of dawn, and any mistakes or mispronunciations will mean that the incantation will fail. If the ritual has been performed correctly, the Tomb Scorpion will become infused with the residual power of the priest held within it. Tomb Scorpions often stand dormant for centuries on end, and become buried by the shifting sands. When the Tomb Kings go to war, the Liche Priests send out their call, and the Tomb Scorpions awake, clawing their way to the surface to fall upon their enemies with mighty claws and stinging tails. It is truly a terrifying sight to behold the sands shift and part as the monstrous creations work their way to the surface!

| | M | WS | BS | S | T | W | I | A | Ld |
|---|---|---|---|---|---|---|---|---|---|
| Tomb Scorpion | 7 | 4 | 0 | 5 | 5 | 4 | 3 | 4 | 8 |

## SPECIAL RULES

**Undead Constructs**

Tomb Scorpions are made in part of resurrected dead creatures and in part of wood, stone and metal, all moulded together by the powerful magic of the Liche Priests. As a result of this, they are more resilient than normal Undead and always count as if they are within 12" of the Battle Standard, even if there is no Battle Standard on the table. If they actually are within 12" of the Battle Standard then they will benefit from that as well, losing two less wounds than they should from lost combats. In addition, Undead Constructs have a 5+ Armour save.

**"It Came From Below..."**

Tomb Scorpions do not have to be deployed at the beginning of the game, and can use the "It Came From Below..." rules given opposite if they choose.

**Poisoned Attacks**

The Tomb Scorpion's tail carries a potent sting that can incapacitate even the largest foes. A Tomb Scorpion has Poisoned Attacks (see page 114 of the Warhammer rulebook). Note that because hits that count as successful Poisoned Attacks do not need to roll to wound, there is no chance of scoring a Killing Blow with them.

**Killing Blow**

The powerful claws of the Tomb Scorpion can slice a man in half, and attacks made by it follow the Killing Blow special rule (see page 112 of the Warhammer rulebook).

**Magic Resistance (1)**

The magical energy for a Tomb Scorpion is provided by the mummified Liche Priest contained within its carapace. This magical source also provides a degree of protection against spells, giving the Tomb Scorpion Magic Resistance (1) as detailed on page 114 of the Warhammer rulebook.

# IT CAME FROM BELOW...

After both sides have set up (including Scouts), place a marker (a coin will do) anywhere on the battlefield for each unit that is entombed in the sands. At the beginning of each Tomb Kings turn, except for the first, roll a D6 to determine if the creatures emerge:

| Turn | Result |
|---|---|
| **First turn:** | N/A |
| **Second turn:** | 4+ to emerge |
| **Third turn:** | 3+ to emerge |
| **Fourth turn:** | 2+ to emerge |
| **Fifth turn:** | Emerge automatically |

When the creatures emerge, roll a Scatter dice and an Artillery dice. If you roll a Hit on the Scatter dice, the marker stays in place; if you roll an arrow, move the marker the distance indicated by the Artillery dice in the direction shown by the arrow.

Once the final position of the marker has been established, replace the marker with one of the emerging unit's models and place all the other models in the unit within 2" of the first one. They emerge at the beginning of the turn (this is the very first thing they do that turn) and can then act normally, and are even allowed to declare a charge!

If the marker is moved under an enemy unit, the emerging Tomb Kings unit will automatically engage it in close combat on the side that is closest to the marker (the Tomb Kings unit counts as charging). If the marker is moved under a friendly unit or impassable terrain, place the Tomb Kings unit on the closest edge of the unit/obstacle. If the marker is moved off the battlefield, they are buried too deep (as per result 3-4 on the Mishap table below).

If you roll a Misfire, roll a D6 and consult the Mishap table below.

### MISHAP TABLE

**D6/Result**

1-2: *Magic Dissipated*
The energy that awakens these creatures dissipates. The emerging models are destroyed and the enemy gets Victory points for their destruction.

3-4: *Too Deep*
Buried far deeper than expected beneath the ground, the creatures fail to burrow their way to the surface in time to take part in the battle. They cannot be used in the battle, but the enemy will not earn Victory points for them.

5-6: *Misaligned*
Your opponent can place the marker anywhere on the battlefield and deploy the emerging unit. The unit cannot move in the Movement phase of the turn it emerges.

# CARRION

"The Carrion of the Desert, whose mighty outstretched wings darken the noon day sun on the day of slaughter."

Part of an invocation chant of the Liche Priests used at the Temple of the Sun in Khemri.

According to inscriptions, King Nekhef claimed to be the first ruler to use Carrion in his army of eternity. These creatures lived in the mountains to the east of Nehekhara and also the deserts to the west. Their broad wings were said to darken the sky, spreading the shadow of doom upon those dying in the desert. After a great battle, with the slain strewn over the stricken field, the Carrion descended and blotted out the light of the sun. Thus it was in ancient Nehekhara that the Carrion was seen as a sacred beast that bore the spirits of slain warriors to the sky to fight in endless battles against the daemons of darkness. This belief led to the priests burying many corpses of Carrion in the necropoli of each Tomb King from the time of Nekhef I onwards. As the revered birds eventually died out, only those that were entombed remained. At the will of the Liche Priests they once again take to the skies, their horrifying forms spreading fear amongst those who feel the chill of their shadow.

| | M | WS | BS | S | T | W | I | A | Ld |
|---|---|---|---|---|---|---|---|---|---|
| Carrion | 2 | 3 | 0 | 3 | 4 | 2 | 3 | 2 | 4 |

## SPECIAL RULES

**Flying Unit**
Carrion are a unit of flyers and follow the rules on page 106 of the Warhammer rulebook.

# BONE GIANT

"That which was stone, arise! Bone and bronze and leather and tar, creature of power awake and visit destruction on the enemies of Khemri!"

Part of the awakening ritual performed by the High Priest Kharnut during the time of the Second Dynasty.

In ancient times, before the rise of the Mortuary Cult, many were the legends of mighty beings of immense stature walking the land and smiting all who stood in their path. As the knowledge and skill of the priesthood grew, they turned their talents towards recreating a being of the size and power that the legends spoke of, for who could face such a creation in battle? Thus the first Bone Giants were painstakingly crafted, formed from all manner of elements and held together by the powerful incantations of the Liche Priests.

Made to resemble an immense warrior of Nehekhara, the Bone Giant is armed with traditional weapons and armour on a mighty scale. It is a rare thing to create a new Bone Giant, and most of those that are at times seen marching to battle alongside the Tomb Kings' armies have been in existence for thousands of years. If one of the constructs is destroyed, its sacred pieces are gathered up and used to recreate it.

Outside the ancient cities of Nehekhara, Bone Giants stand as motionless sentinels, guarding important valley entrances and gateways. Such power is instilled in the Bone Giants that they do not need the incantations of the Liche Priests to prompt them into wakefulness, and will react immediately to the presence of unwelcome strangers, striding relentlessly towards them, smashing them into the sand with their heavy weapons.

| | M | WS | BS | S | T | W | I | A | Ld |
|---|---|---|---|---|---|---|---|---|---|
| Bone Giant | 6 | 3 | 0 | 6 | 5 | 6 | 1 | 4 | 8 |

## SPECIAL RULES

### Undead Construct

A Bone Giant is not the animated skeleton of a single creature, but a massive warrior built from the bones of mighty desert creatures, bound together with wood and metal by the magic of the Liche Priests. As a result of this, they are more resilient than normal Undead and always count as if they are within 12" of the Battle Standard, even if there is no Battle Standard on the table. If they actually are within 12" of the Battle Standard then they will benefit from that as well, losing two less wounds than they should from lost combats.
In addition, Undead Constructs have a 5+ Armour save.

### Terror

Bone Giants are massive, imposing creations, inspiring dread in the hearts of the enemy. They cause *terror* (see page 81 of the Warhammer rulebook).

### Large Target

Bone Giants tower over the Tomb King's legions. They follow the rules for large targets.

### Unstoppable Assault

A charging Bone Giant is a terrifying sight to behold, smashing into the enemy and sending them flying with powerful blows. For every wounding hit that the Bone Giant inflicts when it charges (before saving throws), the Bone Giant gets to make an additional attack. Such additional attacks also benefit from the Unstoppable Assault rule.

# SCREAMING SKULL CATAPULT

"The executioners who decapitate the rebels. They who hurl the wailing heads of the enemies of the king."

Inscription above the tomb pit of the Skull Catapults in Zandri.

It is said that Behedesh, King of Zandri, claimed to have invented this type of catapult and ordered them to be constructed. He used these in his many wars and had them mounted on his numerous war galleys, which gave him domination of the great River Mortis during his mortal lifetime. When he had extended his rule along the western bank of the river, but had yet to subdue the kings and rebels encamped on the eastern bank, he gathered a great many catapults together and hurled over the skulls of his decapitated enemies who had been captured in earlier battles. This demoralised his opponents and caused their army to lose heart when the final onslaught came. The king wished to repeat this tactic again against other, more redoubtable enemies. Therefore he instructed the priests to devise a spell to be written on the skulls of decapitated rebels in hieroglyphic signs that would make the enemy tremble with fear. This the priests demonstrated to the king. They enchanted the skulls so that they screamed hideously as they were hurled through the air – it was the very death scream of the rebel at his moment of execution. The skulls were also daubed in resins that burst into eerie, ethereal flames as they flew. The king was indeed impressed and decreed that henceforth the heads of all rebels would be reserved for these catapults.

When the king was approaching death, he gave instructions that the catapults should be entombed as an essential part of his necropolis army, since they had brought him more than one victory in life and he expected them to do so again beyond death. The successors of Behedesh followed his example. Centuries later, other kings who extended their rule over Zandri ransacked the necropolis and found the burial pits containing the catapults. These were looted and taken away for reburial in other necropoli, together with scrolls containing incantations of awakening and hieroglyphs of enchantment to be inscribed on the skulls.

| | M | WS | BS | S | T | W | I | A | Ld |
|---|---|---|---|---|---|---|---|---|---|
| Catapult | – | – | – | – | 7 | 3 | – | – | – |
| Crew | 4 | 2 | 2 | 3 | 3 | 1 | 2 | 1 | 3 |

## SPECIAL RULES

**Stone Thrower**
The Screaming Skull Catapult operates in exactly the same way as a Stone Thrower (see page 120 of the Warhammer rulebook) except that it hurls screaming skulls instead of rocks.

**Screaming Skulls**
When screaming and flaming skulls land among the enemy it is a very unnerving experience for them! To represent this, any unit that suffers one or more wounds from a shooting attack by a Screaming Skull Catapult must take a Panic test. Because of the weird nature of the screaming skull ammunition, the catapult inflicts magical attacks, which also count as flaming attacks (see page 114 of the Warhammer rulebook).

**Skulls of the Foe**
Screaming Skull Catapults may be upgraded to allow them to hurl the skulls of the race they are fighting. So, a catapult with this upgrade can hurl Orc skulls at Orc enemies, or Dwarfish skulls at Dwarfs. This is even more terrifying than the catapult's usual ammunition, and any unit that must make a Panic test from the Screaming Skull Catapult suffer a -1 to their Leadership.

# CASKET OF SOULS

"Damnation eternal awaits those who would disturb his rest! Here be the souls of those that are lost..."

Inscribed on the Casket of Souls within the tomb of King Setep.

Within the tombs of the mightiest kings there lies a casket sealed with pitch and inscribed with hieroglyphs of malediction and warning. Within this sacred sarcophagus reside the souls of those who have committed the sacrilege of inciting the Tomb King's rage. Whether consumed by ravenous Tomb Swarms or cut down by the Tomb Guard, the spirits of those thus condemned have been ensnared by the dire power of the casket and trapped within it for eternity. Powerful inscriptions ensure that these souls may never leave their binding prison until the moment comes when the casket is opened.

If the seals are broken and the lid opened, blinding light spills from the casket as countless lost souls scream into the air, seeking freedom from the madness and torment of their confinement. Such an escape will never come while the casket is intact, for the pull of the damned sarcophagus is so great that it draws the souls back within no matter how hard they try to fight it. Crazed and desperate, these insubstantial spirits plunge through the hearts and minds of those nearby, hopelessly seeking an escape. As the screaming forms of these souls pass through the physical bodies of living creatures, the life force of that creature is sucked dry. They feel an intense pain deep within them, and their bodies age centuries with every passing second. In mere heartbeats, they are little more than a dried shell and they fall to the ground. Far worse than physical death, those who perish in this manner are condemned in soul as well as body. As their spirit begins to rise from their fallen body, they too become ensnared by the power of the casket, becoming just another of the countless lost souls held within its unholy confines for an eternity of torment. The spirits affect even creatures that do not truly age or have a soul, as the magical energies that bind them together or keep them on this plane of existence are absorbed. Carried onto the field of battle, a Casket of Souls is a devastating weapon, for all who look upon it risk eternal damnation and entrapment.

| | M | WS | BS | S | T | W | I | A | Ld |
|---|---|---|---|---|---|---|---|---|---|
| Casket Guard | 4 | 3 | 3 | 4 | 4 | 1 | 3 | 2 | 8 |

## SPECIAL RULES

**War Machine**
The Casket Guards and Liche Priest/Liche High Priest associated with the Casket act much like a war machine's crew for the Casket of Souls. The Casket of Souls uses the rules for war machines, (see pages 118-119 of the Warhammer rulebook) with the following exceptions:

If, for whatever reason, there is no Liche Priest or Liche High Priest acting as part of the crew for the Casket at the beginning of any Tomb Kings turn, the Casket and its two Casket Guards immediately collapse and are removed from the table.

The Casket of Souls cannot move.

Any hits from shooting that strike the Casket itself are ignored. Hits on the crew are randomised between the Casket's two Guards and any associated Liche Priests or Liche High Priests.

**The Light of Death**
When the souls within the magical casket are unleashed, they erupt in a great burst of light that sears the eyes and flesh of unbelievers who look upon it. The Light of Death is released at the end of the Tomb King's Magic phase, so long as the Casket and its crew are not engaged in combat. It is cast like an incantation (see pages 34-35) with a Power Level of 2D6. If successfully cast, it affects all enemy units that can draw a line of sight to the Casket itself. Roll 2D6+2 and deduct the unit's Leadership from the total. The score is the number of wounds the unit suffers, with no Armour saves allowed, distributed as shooting hits. These hits count as magical attacks. Roll separately for each unit that can see the Casket.

**Spirit-Souls**
The presence of so many tortured souls on the battlefield is particularly disturbing and harrowing for enemy spellcasters. As long as the Casket of Souls is on the table, all enemy Wizards suffer -1 on their total Casting dice roll when casting spells. Note that this will have no effect if an Irresistible Force is rolled and cannot cause a Miscast.

**Terror**
The Casket of Souls is surrounded by an unnatural aura of death and despair. It causes *terror* (see page 81 of the Warhammer rulebook).

**Tomb Blades**
Casket Guards were excellent soldiers during their lives and gifted with weapons that had incantations of cursing imbued into them. Casket Guards have the Killing Blow special rule (see page 112 of the Warhammer rulebook) and their attacks count as magical.

# LICHE PRIEST MAGIC

*This section of the book deals with the spells and magic items of the Tomb Kings army. Tomb Kings magic works very differently to other types of magic, and mastery of its tactical uses is vital to command the legions of Nehekhara.*

The magic of Nehekhara's Liche Priests is based on long, monotonous enchantments that connect the mortal world to the realms beyond. The wording of these arcane spells has been recorded on dusty papyri, written in the mysterious hieroglyphs of Nehekhara's ancient language. These incantations, uttered in rituals unchanged for uncountable millennia, cannot reach the peaks of sheer power achieved by their perverted versions that are the necromantic spells taught by the heretical Nagash to his disciples. On the other hand, they are far more reliable and, when relentlessly intoned in unison by several of the unliving Liche Priests, they are almost unstoppable.

## Using Nehekharan Incantations

Liche Priests and Liche High Priests are treated as Wizards but they don't generate any Power dice. They generate Dispel dice as normal in the enemy Magic phase – one per Priest and two per High Priest.

They always know all four Incantations (see the next page for the Incantations' effects).

A Priest can cast one of the four Incantations in each of his own Magic phases. A High Priest can cast two (or even the same incantation twice).

The incantation chosen is automatically cast like a bound spell, at a Power Level that is determined by rolling 2D6 in the case of a Priest's incantation, and 3D6 in the case of a High Priest. Note that these are not Power dice, and can neither be negated by enemy items, nor stolen or anything similar. Also, Liche Priests cannot take advantage of gaining additional magical power from such things as an enemy Miscast. Items which modify the Power Level of spell rolls do affect Incantations (such as the High Elf spell *Drain Magic*, or the magic item, Amulet of the Purifying Flame).

The rules for Irresistible Force and Miscasts do not apply to Incantations, but the rules for automatic failure do apply to Dispel attempts made in the enemy Magic phase. Also, the spell is always cast unless dispelled by the enemy. For example, even if a roll of 3 or less is made for the Power Level. In all other respects the Incantations are treated as normal spells. For example, if the spell is destroyed by an enemy magic item (such as the Seal of Destruction from the Empire Magic Items list), then the Liche Priest who suffers the effect will not know that incantation for the remainder of the battle.

## Hieratic Hierarchy

At the beginning of the battle assign a hierarchical order to all the Liche Priests in your army. The army's Hierophant is always the most important Priest, and High Priests are always more important than Liche Priests, but apart from these two rules you are free to choose any order you like. Write down the hierarchical order to remember it during the game.

During your Magic phases, the Priests will always perform their role in strict order (ie, do everything they intend to do in that Magic phase: cast their Incantations, use any Bound spell items, etc) from the least important Priest to the Hierophant, in a ritual that has been repeated for scores of centuries.

So always remember to do everything you intend to do with a Priest before you pass to the next in the hierarchic order; once a Priest has finished his actions and another has begun his, there is no going back.

## Order for Magic

There is a strict order in which Tomb Kings magic must be performed.

**1.** All Bound items not used by characters.

**2.** Icon Bearer: Bound Items

**3.** Tomb Princes: "My Will be Done!" and Bound Items

**4.** Tomb Kings: "My Will be Done!" and Bound Items

**5.** Hieratic Hierarchy – Liche Priests and High Liche Priests must use their Bound Items when it is their turn to perform their Incantations.

**6.** The Casket of Souls

# INCANTATIONS

### Sekhubi's Incantation of Vengeance

This is a *magic missile* with a range of 18". If cast, it hits the target and causes D6 Strength 4 hits.

### Horekhah's Incantation of Righteous Smiting

Target one of your own Undead units within 12" of the Priest. If the unit is not engaged in combat, it can immediately shoot with any missile weapons it carries. This is effectively an additional Shooting phase. This can be used on Screaming Skull Catapults too (if they have not moved that turn). As this counts as an additional Shooting phase, an Incantation of Righteous Smiting successfully cast on a unit that could not shoot in its next Shooting phase, due to a misfire or spell for example, may count this as that next Shooting phase. In effect they cannot shoot in this magical Shooting phase, but will be able to then shoot in the regular Shooting phase.

If the unit is engaged in close combat, all models in the unit can immediately make one normal close combat attack against any models they are in base contact with, exactly as they would have done in the following Close Combat phase (including Strength bonuses if charging, etc, but excluding impact hits). In the case of cavalry, both rider and mount may make one attack. For chariots, both steeds and crew can each make one attack. There is no combat resolution, but if enough casualties are caused the enemy unit must take a Panic test. If the enemy unit *panics* and flee, and the Undead are free to move, the Undead must pursue the enemy (they can test to r[illegible]train pursuit as normal).

Units may be affected by this incantation or[illegible]nce per Magic phase, regardless of its source.

### Djedra's Incantation of Summoning

Target one of your own Undead units within 12" of the Priest, even if engaged in combat. If the incantation is successful, warriors that have fallen rise again to fight for their king. The affected unit regains D3 wounds (or D3 wounds worth of models), up to the initial number of wounds on the model's profile or models in the unit. Tomb Guard regain D6 wounds worth of models rather than D3. Skeleton Warriors are easier to resurrect than other Undead, so two D6 may be rolled, and the highest dice roll is the number of wounds worth of models that is regained.

The unit may never have more wounds or models than it started the game with. This can effectively bring back models (including Champions, Musicians and Standard Bearers) that have been killed if their unit still survives and the spell regenerates enough wounds. Any unit in the Tomb Kings army may be healed in this manner, including undead constructs and chariots. For example, the spell is cast on a unit of Ushabti that has already lost two models and another has suffered two wounds. The player rolls a 5, restoring three Wounds, so the wounded model is repaired (two Wounds) and one of the destroyed Ushabti is brought back with a single Wound.

The wounds must be 'healed' in a strict order. First, any Champions will be healed/resurrected and then other command models. Once this has been done, any multiple wound rank and file models will be healed to their starting value, and then any remaining wounds can be used to resurrect destroyed rank and file models.

Rank and file models are added to the front rank until the front rank reaches at least four models. Then, additional models may be added to either the front rank or they can be added to create rear ranks. If the unit already has more than one rank, new models can only be added to rear ranks.

Characters must be nominated separately from a unit if they are to benefit from this incantation. If they are riding a chariot, the player must nominate whether it is the chariot or the character who is going to be healed. Any excess wounds that are not used are lost. In the same manner, war machine crew are nominated separately from any characters that have joined them and the war machine itself.

Models summoned back into a unit that is involved in combat do not count as charging, even if that unit charged into combat that turn.

### Mankara's Incantation of Urgency

Target one of your own Undead units within 12" of the Priest. It cannot be cast on units engaged in combat. The unit can immediately make its normal move, exactly like in the Movement phase (it can wheel, turn, change formation or even reform, etc).

The unit can charge an enemy and the same rules apply as for a normal charge. A unit charged by means of this incantation can react to the charge as normal and must take the appropriate Psychology tests.

Units may be affected by this incantation only once per Magic phase, regardless of its source.

# TREASURES OF THE NECROPOLIS

*You may choose Magic Items for your characters and units from the following list and/or the common Magic Items in the rulebook. Note that Liche Priests and High Priests cannot use Power Stones.*

## COMMON MAGIC ITEMS

**SWORD OF STRIKING** **30 Points**
Weapon; +1 to hit.

**SWORD OF BATTLE** **25 Points**
Weapon; +1 Attack.

**SWORD OF MIGHT** **20 Points**
Weapon; +1 Strength.

**BITING BLADE** **10 Points**
Weapon; -1 Armour save.

**ENCHANTED SHIELD** **10 Points**
Armour; 5+ Armour save.

**TALISMAN OF PROTECTION** **15 Points**
Talisman; 6+ Ward save.

**DISPEL SCROLL** **25 Points**
**One use only**
Arcane; Automatically dispel an enemy spell.

**STAFF OF SORCERY** **50 Points**
Arcane; +1 to dispel.

**WAR BANNER** **25 Points**
Banner; +1 combat resolution.

## MAGIC WEAPONS

**DESTROYER OF ETERNITIES** **70 Points**
**Tomb King on foot only**
*The bloodthirsty King Nekhesh first wielded this massive, ornate blade in battle, smashing his foes in all directions and severing limbs and heads with each swing. It is said that those slain by its blade have no chance of reaching the afterlife, and it was thus greatly feared in ancient Nehekhara. The sword was also used to ritually execute captured foes of the king, and it can cleave through armour, muscle and bone with ease.*

Counts as a great weapon and has the Killing Blow special ability. The player may choose to attack normally with the Destroyer of Eternities or make a special attack. If the special attack is chosen, all enemy models that are touching the Tomb King take two automatic hits. These hits do benefit from the special rules for great weapons and Killing Blow. If a target is riding a monster or a chariot, then both take two automatic hits. In a challenge, only the model engaged in the challenge counts as being in contact with the Tomb King.

**CROOK & FLAIL OF RADIANCE** **50 Points**
**Tomb King or Tomb Prince only.**
*These gleaming, golden weapons represent the high status of the bearer, and all in his presence are humbled by the aura of majesty these weapons convey. Only the most powerful and influential leaders may bear these sacred symbols of rulership.*

+1 Attack. Always strikes first. If another character has this ability, then resolve the order of attacks in Initiative order. Requires two hands.

**BLADE OF SETEP** **50 Points**
*This highly ornamented curved sword belonged to King Setep of the 5th Khemrian Dynasty, and its edge shimmers with blue energy that can shatter armour.*

Normal armour cannot save against the Blade of Setep. If an enemy model hit by this sword wears magical armour, then the first hit is automatically discounted (do not roll to wound) but the magical armour is destroyed for the remainder of the battle. Resolve any further hits as normal.

### THE BLADE OF MOURNING 50 Points

*Forged in the heart of Settra's pyramid on the centenary of the king's death, this blade leaves sorrow and despair in its wake.*

If a unit suffers at least one wound from the Blade and loses the combat, any negative modifiers to the unit's Leadership for the subsequent Break test are doubled.

### FLAIL OF SKULLS 45 Points

*This flail is made from the gilded skulls of conquered enemies. Enemies struck by the skulls are lacerated and savaged by their sharpened teeth, and bleed profusely from their wounds.*

Counts as a flail (see page 91 in the Warhammer rulebook). Each unsaved wound becomes two wounds.

### SPEAR OF ANTARHAK 35 Points

*Forged for the Tomb Prince Antarhak of Numas, this magical spear draws the life energy from the enemy and suffuses the wielder with the stolen essence.*

Follows all of the normal rules for a spear. In addition, for every unsaved wound inflicted by the Spear of Antarhak, either the character, his chariot or a unit he is accompanying immediately regains 1 Wound as if Djedra's Incantation of Summoning has been cast on them. Note that wounds inflicted by the enemy and subsequently healed by the Spear still count for combat resolution.

### SERPENT STAFF 25 Points

**High Liche Priests and Liche Priests only.**

*Crafted in the shape of a cobra, this staff can come to life and strike at its foe with a venomous bite.*

Attacks with the Serpent Staff count as Poisoned Attacks. In addition, the model may re-roll any failed rolls to wound in close combat.

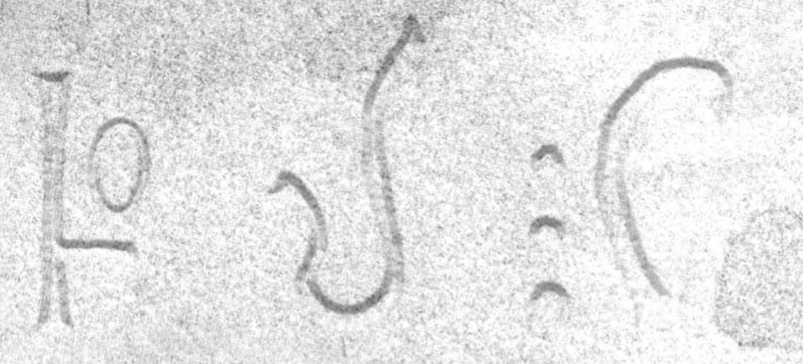

## MAGIC ARMOUR

*Note that High Liche Priests and Liche Priests may not take magic armour.*

### ARMOUR OF ETERNITY 70 Points

*Forged from the bronze of Mahrak, cooled in the blood of the giant Lybrasian scorpion and gilded with red gold from Lahmia, this ancient breastplate can turn aside even the strongest blow.*

Enemy models must re-roll successful rolls to wound against the character. Counts as light armour.

### SCORPION ARMOUR 40 Points

*This armour is decorated with designs of the Scorpion God, and is infused with protective energies.*

The character can never suffer more than one wound due to combat resolution (after any modifiers for being within 12" of the Battle Standard, etc). If the wearer is with a unit, no more than half the wounds suffered due to combat resolution can be allocated against the character. For example, if the unit suffers four wounds, two wounds are lost by the unit and two wounds are allocated to the character of which one is ignored. Counts as heavy armour.

### ARMOUR OF THE AGES 35 Points

*This armour imbues its wearer with the ability to continue fighting even when horrendously injured.*

Counts as heavy armour. The bearer gains +1 Wound.

### SHIELD OF PTRA 15 Points

*This mystical shield contains the energy of the Sun God Ptra, unleashed in a blinding flash of light.*

Counts as a shield. If the bearer makes an Armour save, any enemy unit in base contact reduces its WS to 1 for the remainder of the combat round.

## TALISMANS

### GOLDEN ANKHRA 45 Points

*Shaped in the Nehekharan symbol of eternity, the Ankhra surrounds the wearer with protective energies.*

The model has a 4+ Ward save.

### CROWN OF KINGS 40 Points

**Tomb King only**

*Worn by the rulers of Quatar since the city was founded, the Crown of Kings instils the undying will of the wearer into all those nearby.*

The Crown of Kings enables the Tomb King to roll two D6 for his "My Will Be Done!" incantations and to choose the highest score.

### AMULET OF PHA-STAH 40 Points

*Shaped like the rising moon over the dunes, the Amulet of Pha-stah projects a disruptive magical energy that counters the defences of the foe.*

Any Arcane items, Enchanted items, Talismans or Runic Talismans belonging to enemy models in base contact with the wearer cease to function while they are in base contact.

A character with this item cannot take any other magic items.

## COLLAR OF SHAPESH 25 Points

*This was created by a High Priest of Osir in ancient Kasabar. Its powerful charm protects the wearer from harm, although the god of the Underworld, not to be thwarted, will duly steal the life from another.*

For each wound that the bearer suffers (after saves, etc, but before any multiple wounds are calculated) roll a D6. On a 4+ the wound is transferred to any friendly model within 4" of the bearer's choosing. If inflicted in combat, these wounds will still count for combat resolution. This second model may not make any Armour save or Ward save to avoid this automatic wound. If there is no friendly model within range, then the Collar of Shapesh has no effect.

## GOLDEN EYE OF RAH-NUTT 25 Points

**Character in chariot only.**

*This sigil was carved into the war chariot of the Tomb King Rah-nutt, and imbued his chariot with great power. It is said that arrows and spears bounced off the chariot's sides as Rah-nutt rode into battle.*

The chariot itself gains a Ward save of 5+, which only works against hits struck against the chariot, and will not apply to the character. In addition, wounding hits of Strength 7 or more that would normally destroy the chariot automatically do normal damage instead.

# ENCHANTED ITEMS

## BLUE KHEPRA 40 Points

*Fashioned from exotic sapphires and crafted in the shape of the flesh-eating, skull-carapaced Khepra beetle, this ornate brooch protects the wearer from baleful magical energy.*

The bearer and the unit he joins have Magic Resistance (2).

## DEATH MASK OF KHARNUT 35 Points

*The expressionless, gold Death Mask of Kharnut has witnessed the doom of thousands over the centuries, and the taint of death hangs heavy upon it.*

A model wearing this mask causes *terror*.

## BROOCH OF THE GREAT DESERT 25 Points

**One use only.**

*Inlaid with gold and lapis lazuli, this brooch was first used against the foul necromancy of Nagash, hampering the effectiveness of his dark magic. Each time it is used, its powers are drained, requiring careful incantations from the Liche Priests to restore it to full effect.*

As soon as an enemy spell is cast, the Brooch of the Great Desert may be used to automatically dispel it, just like a Dispel Scroll. Note that as with Dispel Scrolls, the Brooch cannot be used to dispel a spell that is cast with Irresistible Force.

## CHARIOT OF FIRE 25 Points

**Character in chariot only.**

*The wheels and scythes of the mighty hero's chariot blaze with mystical flames.*

The character's chariot does D6+1 impacts hits, rather than D3. Impact hits from the Chariot of Fire count as both magical attacks and flaming attacks.

## CLOAK OF THE DUNES 20 Points

**Characters on foot only**

*Bound with the magic of the deserts, the cloak enables the wearer to transform into a whirling cloud of sand and move rapidly across the battlefield.*

The character can move as if flying, but may not charge whilst using this special movement. He pursues 3D6".

## ICON OF RULERSHIP 20 Points

**Character in chariot only.**

*The hero's chariot carries a mighty totemic pole proclaiming his victories over the enemies of the Tomb Kings, that pulses with an aura of greatness.*

May be taken in addition to another item in the Enchanted Items list. The character's chariot has +1 Unit Strength (so will be worth a total Unit Strength of 5).

## VAMBRACES OF THE SUN 15 Points

*These ancient armbands of intricately decorated bronze are infused with the intensity of the sun. In battle, this harnessed power dazzles the wearer's opponents.*

One model in base contact, chosen by the bearer, loses 1 Attack. Against mounted models, the Tomb Kings player must choose either the mount/monster or the rider. If the model has several types of attack, the Tomb Kings player chooses which type of attack is lost. This has no effect against foes which do not use their Attacks value in combat, such as Giants.

# ARCANE ITEMS

## STAFF OF RAVENING 45 Points

**Bound Item, Power Level 4**

*This staff unleashes the power of the famine-bringing locusts of Nehekhara, and they descend on the foes of the Tomb Kings in a frenzied cloud.*

This spell is a *magic missile* with 18" range. The targeted unit suffers 3D6 Strength 2 hits.

## NEFERRA'S PLAQUES OF MIGHTY INCANTATIONS 30 Points

*Neferra, High Priestess to King Khutef, committed her knowledge to enchanted tablets so that it would never be lost.*

The Priest may re-roll the dice rolled for any Incantation he's cast. Either all of the dice must be re-rolled or none.

### STAFF OF MASTERY 40 Points

*Wielded by Amon-Shapa in the time before the Great Awakening, this copper staff draws magical energy from the Wind of Light to power the Liche Priest's spells.*

The bearer adds +1 to the total rolled to determine the Power Level of his incantations.

### HIERATIC JAR 25 Points

**One use only.**

*This earthenware container is sealed and bound with glyphs of power. Inside are the remains of a Liche Priest who has finally succumbed to the march of time, and it is a potent source of magical energy.*

The Liche Priest may release the energy of the Hieratic Jar during any Magic phase, just after he has cast his normal incantation(s). The Jar allows him to use an extra incantation that phase.

### ENKHIL'S KANOPI 20 Points

**Bound Item, Power Level 4.**

*Within this inauspicious clay vessel is the ancient heart of High Priest Enkhil, removed from his body when he was embalmed and entombed. A jealous and powerful priest when alive, his essence continues within his heart. When opened, it sucks the swirling magic energy from the air, drawing the power into the vessel itself.*

If activated successfully, all Remains in Play spells on the tabletop are automatically dispelled.

## MAGIC BANNERS

### STANDARD OF THE SANDS 75 Points

**One use only.**

*Created for the famed general Amenemhetum the Great, this banner summons a raging storm of sand that sweeps over the battlefield. With screaming winds and biting sand assaulting them, the enemies of the Tomb Kings become momentarily disorientated and confused.*

At the start of any of your opponent's turns, the Standard of the Sands may be activated. The opponent may not make any march moves (even Dwarfs!) during the Movement phase of that turn, although skirmishers and man-sized single models on foot may move as normal. In addition, all units attempting to rally suffer -1 to their Leadership for that player's turn only.

### BANNER OF THE HIDDEN DEAD 60 Points

**One use only.**

*Belonging to the fabled Legion of Hawks, the elite guard of Settra before his mummification, the Banner of the Hidden Dead summons one of his regiments from their honoured place in the Underworld.*

At the beginning of the game, nominate one unit within your army that is to be hidden beneath the ground. This unit must be a Core Unit choice, and cannot cost more than 100 points. This unit is not deployed at the beginning of the game. The banner may be used to unearth the unit during the remaining moves part of any Tomb Kings Movement phase. The entire unit must be placed within 18" of the Banner and at least 1" away from any enemy models. It may move normally on the turn it appears.

### ICON OF THE SACRED EYE 50 Points

*The arcane power of this stylised icon of the unblinking eye infuses the unit that carries it within their ranks, making their blows strike true.*

In the first round of every combat, all models in the unit (including steeds) get +1 to hit.

### MIRAGE STANDARD 40 Points

*Imbued with the curses of a hundred Nehekharan widows, this banner leads the enemies' minds astray, rendering them almost blind to where the unit bearing the banner actually is.*

Any missile weapons that roll to hit must re-roll all successful rolls to hit when firing against a unit that contains the Mirage Standard. Against missile weapons that do not require a roll to hit (such as cannons and stone throwers), all models in the unit containing the Mirage Standard gain a 5+ Ward save.

### ICON OF RAKAPH 40 Points

**Tomb Guard or Skeleton Warriors only.**

*King Rakaph II was an unparalleled tactician. Troops fighting under his banner are instilled with unmatched discipline.*

A unit of Tomb Guard or Skeleton Warriors containing this banner may make a free reform move at the start of its Movement phase. This is done before charges are declared, so that a unit with the Icon of Rakaph may charge on the turn it reforms.

### STANDARD OF THE CURSING WORD 25 Points

*This magic icon contains a powerful curse similar to that which protects the Tomb Kings and Princes in their eternal slumber.*

Each enemy model in base contact with the Standard Bearer at the start of the Tomb Kings' Magic phase must pass a Leadership test (on their own unmodified Ld) or lose a wound (with no Armour save allowed).

### BANNER OF THE UNDYING LEGION 25 Points

**Bound Spell, Power Level 3.**

*This great standard was once the ornamental decoration above the tomb of King Lahmizzar's Jackal Legion. Now it contains the power to restore the fallen.*

Casts Djedra's Incantation of Summoning. May only be cast on the unit containing the banner.

# ARMIES OF KHEMRI

The purpose of an army list is to enable players with vastly different armies to stage games which are as fair and evenly balanced as it is possible to make them. The army list gives each individual model a points value which represents its capabilities on the tabletop. The higher a model's points value, the better it is in one or more respects: stronger, tougher, faster, better Leadership, and so on. The value of the army is simply the value of all the models added together.

As well as providing points costs, the list also divides the army into its constituent units. The list describes the weapons and optional equipment that troops can have and occasionally restricts the number of very powerful units an army can include. It would be very silly indeed if an army were to consist entirely of Screaming Skull Catapults, or monstrous Bone Giants. The resulting game would be a frustrating and unbalanced affair, if not a complete waste of time. We employ army lists to ensure that this does not happen!

## USING THE ARMY LIST

The army lists enable two players to choose armies of equal points value to fight a battle, as described in the main body of the Warhammer rules. The following list has been constructed with this purpose in mind.

The list can also be used when playing specific scenarios, either those described in the Warhammer rulebook, or others, including ones invented by the players. In this case, the list provides a framework which the players can adapt as required. It might, for example, be felt necessary to increase or decrease the number of characters or units allowed, or to restrict or remove options in the standard list such as magic items or monstrous mounts. If you refer to the Scenarios section of the Warhammer rulebook (pages 196-213), you'll find some examples of this kind.

## ARMY LIST ORGANISATION

The army list is divided into four sections:

### Characters

Characters represent the most able, skilled and successful individuals in your army: extraordinary leaders such as Tomb Kings and Liche Priests. These form a vital and potent part of your forces.

### Core Units

These units are the most common warriors. They usually form the bulk of the army and will often bear the brunt of the fighting.

### Special Units

Special units are the best of your warriors and include the more unusual troop types. They are available to your army in limited numbers.

### Rare Units

Rare units are so called because they are scarce compared to your ordinary troops. They represent unique units and unusual machines of war.

## Choosing an Army

Both players choose armies to the same agreed points value. Most players find that 2,000 points is about right for a battle that will last over an evening. Whatever value you agree, this is the maximum number of points you can spend. You can spend less and will probably find it is impossible to use up every last point. Most 2,000 points armies will therefore be something like 1,998 or 1,999 points, but they are still '2,000' points armies for our purposes.

Once you have decided on a total points value, it is time to choose your force.

## Choosing Characters

Characters are divided into two broad categories: Lords (the most powerful characters) and Heroes (the rest). The maximum number of characters an army can include is shown on the chart below.

| Army Points Value | Max. Total Characters | Max. Lords | Max. Heroes |
|---|---|---|---|
| Less than 2,000 | 3 | 0 | 3 |
| 2,000 or more | 4 | 1 | 4 |
| 3,000 or more | 6 | 2 | 6 |
| 4,000 or more | 8 | 3 | 8 |
| Each +1,000 | +2 | +1 | +2 |

An army does not have to include the maximum number of characters allowed; it can always include fewer than indicated. **However, an army must always include at least one character: the General.** An army does not have to include Lords, it can include all of its characters as Heroes if you prefer. At the start of the battle, choose one of your Tomb Kings or Tomb Princes to be the General and make sure you let your opponent know which one it is. One Liche Priest or High Priest must also be chosen as the Hierophant.

For example, a 2,500 points army could include a Tomb King (Lord), an Icon Bearer (Hero), a Liche Priest (Hero), and a Tomb Prince (Hero) (ie, four characters in total, of which one is a Lord).

## Choosing Troops

Troops are divided into Core, Special and Rare units. The number of each type of unit available depends on the army's points value, indicated on the chart below.

| Army Points Value | Core Units | Special Units | Rare Units |
|---|---|---|---|
| Less than 2,000 | 2+ | 0-3 | 0-1 |
| 2,000 or more | 3+ | 0-4 | 0-2 |
| 3,000 or more | 4+ | 0-5 | 0-3 |
| 4,000 or more | 5+ | 0-6 | 0-4 |
| Each +1,000 | +1 minimum | +0-1 | +0-1 |

In some cases other limitations may apply to a particular kind of unit. This is specified in the unit entry. For example, the Tomb Swarm Common unit entry is accompanied by a note (ie, 0-1) explaining that a maximum of one unit of this kind can be included in the army.

## Unit Entries

Each unit is represented by an entry in the army list. The unit's name is given and any limitations that apply are explained.

**Profiles.** The characteristic profiles for the troops in each unit are given in the unit entry. Where several profiles are required, these are also given even if, as in many cases, they are optional.

**Unit Sizes.** Each entry specifies the minimum size for each unit. In the case of Core units this is usually 10 models. In the case of other units it is usually less. There are exceptions as you will see. In some cases, units also have a maximum size.

**Weapons and Armour.** Each entry lists the standard weapons and armour for that unit type. The value of these items is included in the points value. Additional or optional weapons and armour cost extra and are covered in the Options section of the unit entry.

**Options.** Lists the different weapon, armour and equipment options for the unit and any additional points cost for taking them. It may also include the option to upgrade a unit member into a Champion. See the appropriate section of the Warhammer rulebook for details (pages 108-109).

**Special Rules.** Many troops have special rules which are fully described elsewhere in this book. These rules are also summarised for your convenience in the army list.

It would be a long and tedious business to repeat all the special rules for every unit within the army list itself. The army list is intended primarily as a tool for choosing armies rather than for presenting game rules. Wherever possible we have indicated where special rules apply and, where space permits, we have provided notes within the list as 'memory joggers'. Bear in mind that these descriptions are not necessarily exhaustive or definitive and players should refer to the main rules for a full account.

## Dogs of War

Dogs of War are troops of other races prepared to fight in return for money, food, or some other reward. The most common type of Dogs of War units are the Regiments of Renown. Although the two terms are used to describe mercenary units, both work in the same way in the army list.

A selection of such regiments is available as part of the Dogs of War range of models. The descriptions and rules for these units can be found in White Dwarf magazine and are compiled in the Warhammer Annual.

The rules for individual Regiments of Renown detail exactly which armies may take them and which army list choices they use up. Most Dogs of War units take up a Rare choice, but some count as Special choices, or may take up more than one choice. This is detailed in the individual rules of the unit itself.

# LORDS

Tomb Kings are the most powerful and ancient characters in the army, and are difficult to destroy. Liche High Priests can cast several incantations each turn, and wield the most powerful mag.

The total number of Lords you can field in your army can be found on page 40.

### + General & Hierophant

Your army must include at least one Tomb King or Prince to be its General, and at least one Liche Priest or Liche High Priest to be the army's Hierophant.

### Skeletal Steed

A Liche Priest and Liche High Priest may ride a Skeletal Steed with the following profile:

| M | WS | BS | S | T | W | I | A | Ld |
|---|---|---|---|---|---|---|---|---|
| 8 | 2 | 0 | 3 | 3 | 1 | 2 | 1 | 5 |

## TOMB KING +

***Points/model: 170***

| | M | WS | BS | S | T | W | I | A | Ld |
|---|---|---|---|---|---|---|---|---|---|
| Tomb King | 4 | 6 | 4 | 5 | 5 | 4 | 3 | 4 | 10 |

**Weapons & Armour:** Hand weapon.

**Options:**

- May choose either a great weapon (+6 pts) or a flail (+3 pts). May choose a spear (+3 pts) if riding in a chariot.
- May wear light armour (+3 pts) and/or carry a shield (+3 pts).
- May ride in a Chariot (+45 pts, see entry in the Core units section of the army list), displacing both Skeleton crew.
- May choose magic items from the Common or Tomb Kings magic items list to a maximum total value of 100 pts.

**Special Rules**

***Undead, Embalmed, The Curse, "My Will Be Done!".***

## LICHE HIGH PRIEST +

***Points/model: 245***

| | M | WS | BS | S | T | W | I | A | Ld |
|---|---|---|---|---|---|---|---|---|---|
| Liche High Priest | 4 | 3 | 3 | 3 | 3 | 3 | 2 | 1 | 9 |

**Weapons & Armour:** Hand weapon.

**Magic:** A Liche High Priest is a Wizard.
He always uses Nehekharan incantations (see pages 34-35).

**Options:**

- May be mounted on a Skeletal Steed for +12 pts.
- May choose magic items from the Common or Tomb Kings magic items list to a maximum total value of 100 pts.
- May choose to take a Casket of Souls to battle (+165 pts). Only one Casket of Souls may be fielded in an army. Choosing the Casket of Souls also uses up a Rare unit choice.

**Special Rules**

***Undead.***

## 0-1 CASKET OF SOULS

***Points/model: 165***

*A Liche Priest/Liche High Priest may be accompanied by a Casket of Souls. Choosing the Casket of Souls also uses up a Rare unit choice.*

| | M | WS | BS | S | T | W | I | A | Ld |
|---|---|---|---|---|---|---|---|---|---|
| Casket Guard | 4 | 3 | 3 | 4 | 4 | 1 | 3 | 2 | 8 |

**Unit Size:** 1

**Crew:** 2 Casket Guards.

**Weapons & Armour:** Casket Guards are armed with great weapons and light armour.

**Special Rules**

**Casket of Souls:** *Terror, Light of Death, Spirit-Souls.*

**Casket Guard:** *Undead, Tomb Blades.*

## TOMB PRINCE ✝ 

***Points/model: 100***

| | M | WS | BS | S | T | W | I | A | Ld |
|---|---|---|---|---|---|---|---|---|---|
| Tomb Prince | 4 | 5 | 4 | 4 | 5 | 3 | 3 | 3 | 9 |

**Weapons & Armour:** Hand weapon.

**Options:**

- May choose either a great weapon (+4 pts), or a flail (+2 pts). May instead choose a spear (+2 pts) if riding in a chariot.
- May wear light armour (+2 pts) and/or carry a shield (+2 pts).
- May ride in a chariot (+45 pts, see entry in the Core Units section of the army list), displacing both Skeleton crew.
- May choose magic items from the Common or Tomb Kings magic items list to a maximum total value of 50 pts.

**Special Rules**

***Undead, Embalmed, The Curse, "My Will Be Done!".***

## 0-1 ICON BEARER

***Points/model: 65***

| | M | WS | BS | S | T | W | I | A | Ld |
|---|---|---|---|---|---|---|---|---|---|
| Icon Bearer | 4 | 4 | 3 | 4 | 4 | 2 | 3 | 2 | 8 |

**Weapons & Armour:** Hand weapon.

**Icon Bearer:** Carries the army's Battle Standard.

**Options:**

- May wear light armour (+2 pts).
- May ride in a chariot (+45 pts, see entry in the Core units section of the army list), displacing both Skeleton crew, or be mounted on a Skeletal Steed (+8 pts).
- May choose magic items from the Common or Tomb Kings magic items list to a maximum total value of 50 pts. Alternatively, he can choose a magic banner (no points limit).

**Special Rules**

***Tomb Blades, Undead.***

## LICHE PRIEST ✝

***Points/model: 115***

| | M | WS | BS | S | T | W | I | A | Ld |
|---|---|---|---|---|---|---|---|---|---|
| Liche Priest | 4 | 3 | 3 | 3 | 3 | 2 | 2 | 1 | 8 |

**Weapons:** Hand weapon.

**Magic:** A Liche Priest is a Wizard.
He always uses Nehekharan incantations (see pages 34-35).

**Options:**

- May be mounted on a Skeletal Steed for +8 pts.
- May choose magic items from the Common or Tomb Kings magic items list to a maximum total value of 50 pts.
- May choose to take a Casket of Souls to battle (+165 pts). Only one Casket of Souls may be fielded in an army. Choosing the Casket of Souls also uses up a Rare unit choice.

**Special Rules**

***Undead.***

# HEROES

The Heroes of the Tomb Kings are powerful individuals who can boost the strength of the units in your army, whether through sheer fighting power (Tomb Princes), magic (Liche Priests), or the enhancement of a Battle Standard (Icon Bearer).

The total number of Heroes you can field in your army can be found on page 40.

# CORE UNITS

Core units are the most numerous troops within the Tomb Kings army, and they represent the loyal soldiers who serve their lord even after death has claimed them.

There is a minimum number of Core units that must be fielded, and this varies depending on the size of the army (see page 41).

There is no maximum limit on the number of Core units that can be fielded.

## SKELETON WARRIORS *Points/model: 8*

| | M | WS | BS | S | T | W | I | A | Ld |
|---|---|---|---|---|---|---|---|---|---|
| Skeleton | 4 | 2 | 2 | 3 | 3 | 1 | 2 | 1 | 3 |
| Champion | 4 | 2 | 2 | 3 | 3 | 1 | 2 | 2 | 3 |

**Unit Size:** 10-40

**Weapons & Armour:** Hand weapon, bow.

**Options:**

- Any unit may replace their bows with shields at no extra cost.
- Any unit may be equipped with light armour (+1 pt/model).
- Any unit may replace their bows with spears and shields (+1 pt/model).
- Any unit may upgrade one Warrior to a Musician for +5 pts.
- Any unit may upgrade one Warrior to a Standard Bearer for +10 pts.
- Any unit may upgrade one Warrior to a Champion for +10 pts.
- If the General is a Tomb King, one unit may be equipped with a magic standard worth up to 25 pts.

**Special Rules**

***Undead.***

## SKELETON LIGHT HORSEMEN *Points/model: 14*

| | M | WS | BS | S | T | W | I | A | Ld |
|---|---|---|---|---|---|---|---|---|---|
| Skeleton | 4 | 2 | 2 | 3 | 3 | 1 | 2 | 1 | 5 |
| Champion | 4 | 2 | 2 | 3 | 3 | 1 | 2 | 2 | 5 |
| Skeletal Steed | 8 | 2 | 0 | 3 | 3 | 1 | 2 | 1 | 5 |

**Unit Size:** 5-16

**Weapons & Armour:** Hand weapon, bow.

**Options:**

- Any unit may upgrade one Warrior to a Musician for +7 pts.
- Any unit may upgrade one Warrior to a Standard Bearer for +14 pts.
- Any unit may upgrade one Warrior to a Champion for +14 pts.

**Special Rules**

***Undead, Fast Cavalry.***

## 0-1 TOMB SWARM *Points/base: 45*

| | M | WS | BS | S | T | W | I | A | Ld |
|---|---|---|---|---|---|---|---|---|---|
| Tomb Swarm | 4 | 3 | 0 | 2 | 2 | 5 | 1 | 5 | 10 |

**Unit Size:** 1-5 bases.

**Weapons & Armour:** None.

**Special Rules**

***Undead, Swarm, Small, Skirmishers, Poisoned Attacks, "It Came From Below...".***

## SKELETON HEAVY HORSEMEN *Points/model: 16*

| | M | WS | BS | S | T | W | I | A | Ld |
|---|---|---|---|---|---|---|---|---|---|
| Skeleton | 4 | 2 | 2 | 3 | 3 | 1 | 2 | 1 | 5 |
| Champion | 4 | 2 | 2 | 3 | 3 | 1 | 2 | 2 | 5 |
| Skeletal Steed | 8 | 2 | 0 | 3 | 3 | 1 | 2 | 1 | 5 |

**Unit Size:** 5-16

**Weapons & Armour:** Hand weapon, spear, light armour and shield.

**Options:**

- Any unit may upgrade one Warrior to a Musician for +7 pts.
- Any unit may upgrade one Warrior to a Standard Bearer for +14 pts.
- Any unit may upgrade one Warrior to a Champion for +14 pts.
- One unit may carry a magic standard worth up to 25 pts.

**Special Rules**

***Undead.***

## CHARIOTS ++ *Points/model: 40*

| | M | WS | BS | S | T | W | I | A | Ld |
|---|---|---|---|---|---|---|---|---|---|
| Chariot | – | – | – | 4 | 4 | 3 | – | – | – |
| Skeleton | – | 3 | 2 | 3 | – | – | 2 | 1 | 7 |
| Champion | – | 3 | 2 | 3 | – | – | 2 | 2 | 7 |
| Skeletal Steed | 8 | 2 | – | 3 | – | – | 2 | 1 | – |

**Unit Size:** 3-12

**Crew:** 1 Skeleton Driver, 1 Skeleton Warrior.

**Chariot Steeds:** 2 Skeleton Steeds.

**Armour Save:** 5+

**Weapons & Armour:** The Skeleton Driver has a hand weapon. The Skeleton Warrior has a hand weapon, spear and bow.

**Options:**

- Any unit may upgrade one Warrior to a Musician for +10 pts.
- Any unit may upgrade one Warrior to a Standard Bearer for +20 pts.
- Any unit may upgrade one Warrior to a Champion for +20 pts.
- One unit may carry a magic standard worth up to 50 pts.

**Special Rules**

***Light Chariots, Undead.***

# CORE UNITS

### ++ Chariots

If your army is led by a Tomb King then Chariots count as Core unit choices. If your army is led by a Tomb Prince, Chariots count as Special unit choices instead.

# SPECIAL UNITS

Special units include elite fighters, specialised creations and undead creatures that appear on the battlefield with less frequency or in fewer numbers than basic troops.

## CHARIOTS

If your army is led by a Tomb King then Chariots count as Core unit choices. If your army is led by a Tomb Prince, Chariots count as Special unit choices instead. See the previous page for the Chariots unit entry.

## TOMB GUARD

***Points/model: 12***

| | M | WS | BS | S | T | W | I | A | Ld |
|---|---|---|---|---|---|---|---|---|---|
| Guard | 4 | 3 | 3 | 4 | 4 | 1 | 3 | 1 | 8 |
| Champion | 4 | 3 | 3 | 4 | 4 | 1 | 3 | 2 | 8 |

**Unit Size:** 10-25

**Weapons & Armour:** Hand weapon, light armour and shield.

**Options:**

- Any unit may upgrade one Guard to a Musician for +6 pts.
- Any unit may upgrade one Guard to a Standard Bearer for +12 pts.
- Any unit may upgrade one Guard to a Champion for +12 pts.
- A Standard Bearer may carry a magic standard worth up to 50 pts.

**Special Rules**

***Tomb Blades, Undead.***

## USHABTI

***Points/model: 65***

| | M | WS | BS | S | T | W | I | A | Ld |
|---|---|---|---|---|---|---|---|---|---|
| Ushabti | 5 | 4 | 0 | 6 | 4 | 3 | 3 | 3 | 10 |

**Unit Size:** 3+

**Weapons:** Huge ritual blades.

**Special Rules**

***Undead Constructs.***

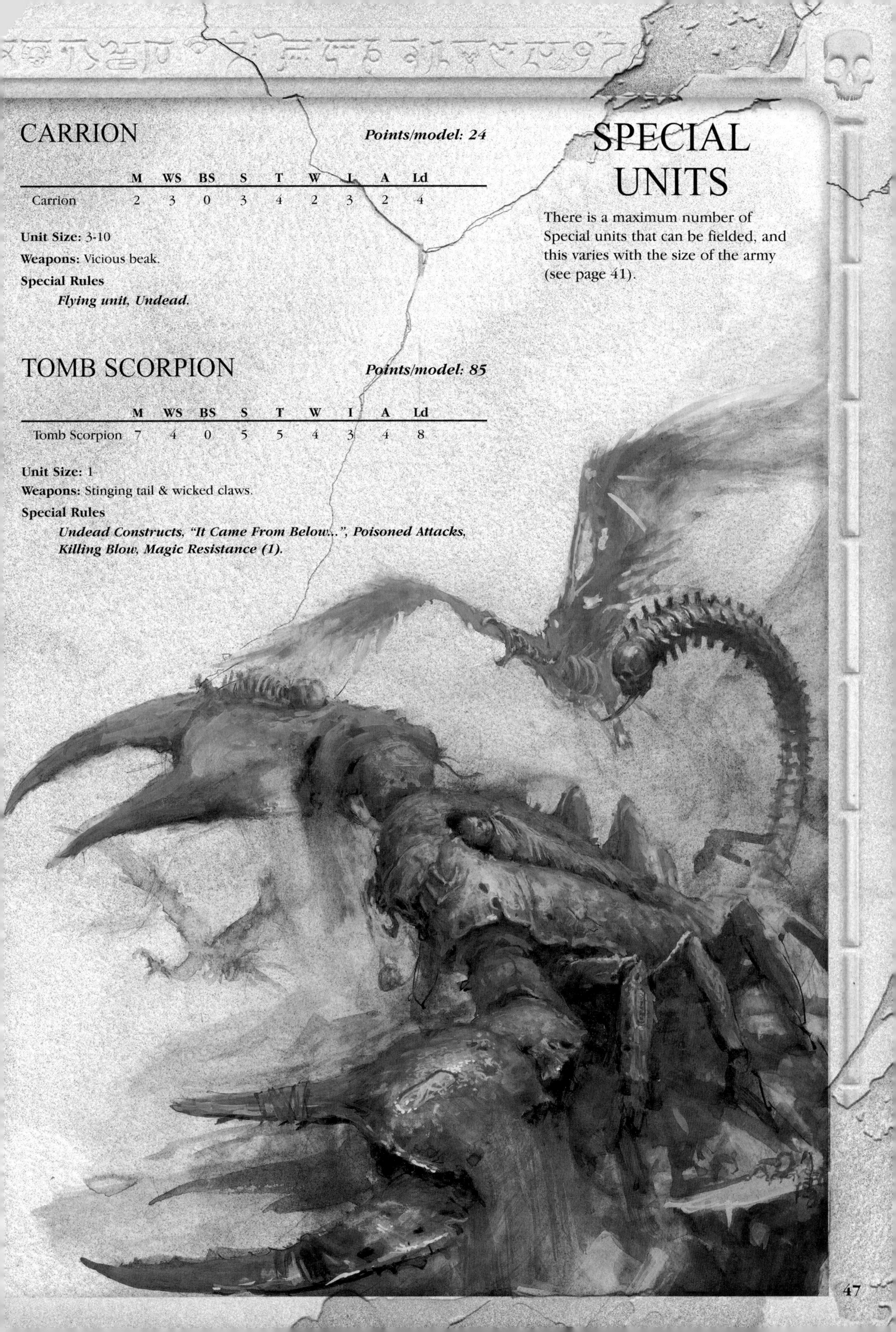

## CARRION

***Points/model: 24***

| | M | WS | BS | S | T | W | I | A | Ld |
|---|---|---|---|---|---|---|---|---|---|
| Carrion | 2 | 3 | 0 | 3 | 4 | 2 | 3 | 2 | 4 |

**Unit Size:** 3-10

**Weapons:** Vicious beak.

**Special Rules**

***Flying unit, Undead.***

## TOMB SCORPION

***Points/model: 85***

| | M | WS | BS | S | T | W | I | A | Ld |
|---|---|---|---|---|---|---|---|---|---|
| Tomb Scorpion | 7 | 4 | 0 | 5 | 5 | 4 | 3 | 4 | 8 |

**Unit Size:** 1

**Weapons:** Stinging tail & wicked claws.

**Special Rules**

***Undead Constructs, "It Came From Below...", Poisoned Attacks, Killing Blow, Magic Resistance (1).***

# SPECIAL UNITS

There is a maximum number of Special units that can be fielded, and this varies with the size of the army (see page 41).

# RARE UNITS

Rare units are some of the most powerful and dangerous creations in the armies of the Tomb Kings. The limited numbers of Bone Giants and Screaming Skull Catapults on the battlefield represent their scarcity.

There is a maximum number of Rare units that can be fielded in an army, and this varies depending on the size of the army (see page 41).

## SCREAMING SKULL CATAPULT

***Points/model:* 90**

| | M | WS | BS | S | T | W | I | A | Ld |
|---|---|---|---|---|---|---|---|---|---|
| Catapult | – | – | – | – | 7 | 3 | – | – | – |
| Skeleton | 4 | 2 | 2 | 3 | 3 | 1 | 2 | 1 | 3 |

**Unit Size:** 1

**Crew:** 3 Skeletons.

**Weapons & Armour:** The Skeleton crew have hand weapons.

**Options:**

- May be upgraded with Skulls of the Foe for +20 points.

**Special Rules**

***Stone Thrower, Screaming Skulls, Undead, Skulls of the Foe.***

## BONE GIANT

***Points/model:* 220**

| | M | WS | BS | S | T | W | I | A | Ld |
|---|---|---|---|---|---|---|---|---|---|
| Bone Giant | 6 | 3 | 0 | 6 | 5 | 6 | 1 | 4 | 8 |

**Unit Size:** 1

**Weapons & Armour:** Two hand weapons, heavy armour (total Armour save 3+).

**Special Rules**

***Undead Construct, Large Target, Terror, Unstoppable Assault.***

## DOGS OF WAR

***Points/model:* *Variable***

*Dogs of War are mercenary units which you can hire to supplement your army. You may choose a unit of Dogs of War as detailed in the Dogs of War rules.*

KING NEKHESH OF THE FIRST DYNASTY STANDS VICTORIOUS IN THE VALLEY OF THE KINGS.

# COLLECTING A TOMB KINGS ARMY

The backbone of the Tomb Kings army consists of large units of Skeletons, and it is an easy army to paint once the general principles of painting bone have been learned. Although the army can consist of a large number of models, Skeletons are relatively easy to assemble and can be painted in large numbers very quickly. Once you have found a technique for painting bone that you are happy with, painting the army is simple. On the other hand, those who enjoy wielding a brush long into the early hours of the morning will find plenty of variety and detail to challenge their skills. With just a little bit of thought it is easy to make your own Tomb Kings force unique, as we have attempted to demonstrate on the pages that follow.

No matter whether the Tomb Kings army is your first army or the latest of several, we hope that the examples and suggestions presented here will both inspire and inform. Whether you choose a simple approach or try to add an amazing level of detail, you can be confident of having one of the most disciplined and fearsome armies there is.

*Skeleton Warriors* *Tomb King*

*Skeleton Chariot*

*Liche Priest*

*Skeleton Warriors with bows*

# PAINTING BONE

**Almost everything in the Tomb Kings army can be painted with the same technique to achieve a bone effect. Here are some ways to do it.**

By far the simplest method to paint bone is to use a Skull White undercoat as a basecoat colour, then apply an ink wash to provide shading and finish off with a drybrush of a lighter colour.

In the example shown to the right, we used a wash of Brown Ink and then drybrushed the Skeleton with Bleached Bone.

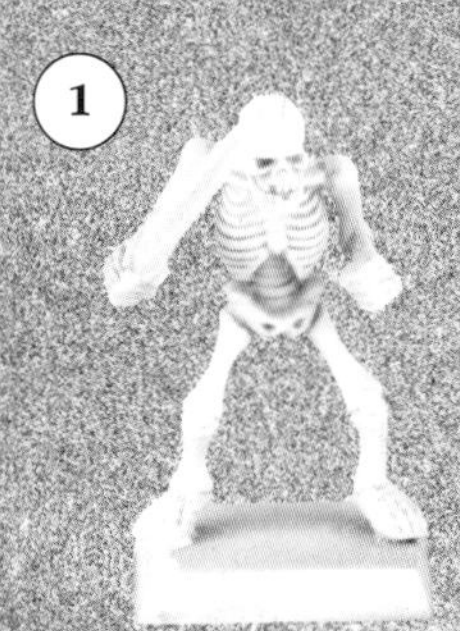

1 Undercoat the model with a Skull White spray.

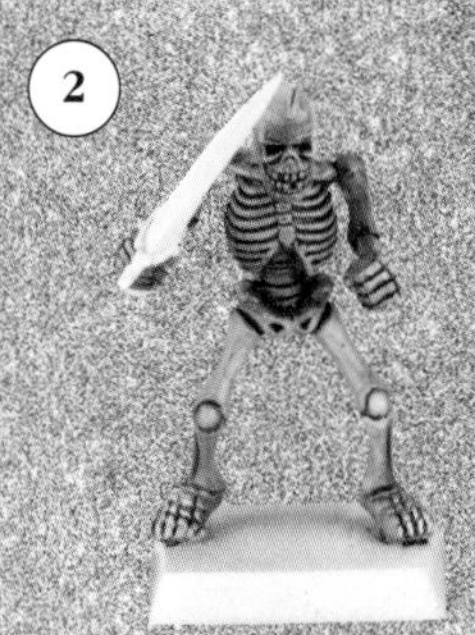

2 Apply a wash of Brown Ink that has been thinned with an equal quantity of water.

3 Drybrush the entire model with Bleached Bone.

## SUGGESTED PAINT COLOURS

- *Undercoat with Skull White*
- *Wash with Black Ink*
- *Drybrush with Skull White*

- *Undercoat with Skull White*
- *Wash with Flesh Wash*
- *Drybrushed with Bleached Bone.*

- *Undercoat with Chaos Black*
- *Drybrush with Bronzed Flesh.*
- *Wash with Brown Ink*
- *Highlight with Bleached Bone*

*We painted our shields Hawk Turquoise as a striking contrast colour to the bone.*

### Shields

Shields are a prominent part of the Tomb Kings army and can be used to make your army look unique and to differentiate between units. Using colours that contrast with the bone that makes up most of the force will help your models stand out on the battlefield. We have used a simple colour scheme for our army but, as the examples below show, you can also use more complex patterns.

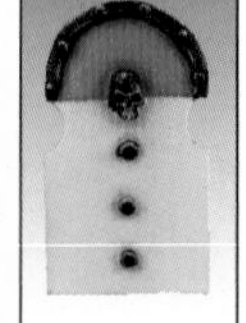
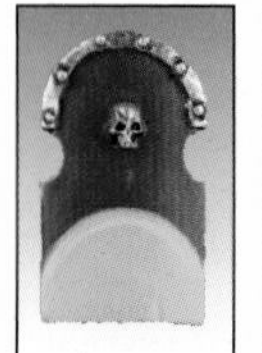
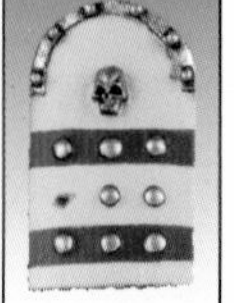

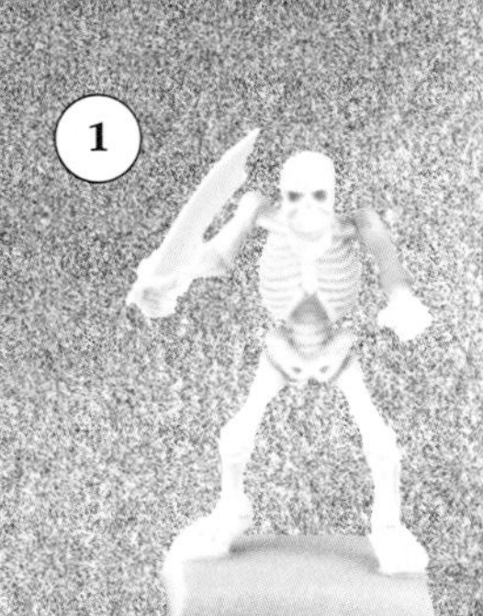

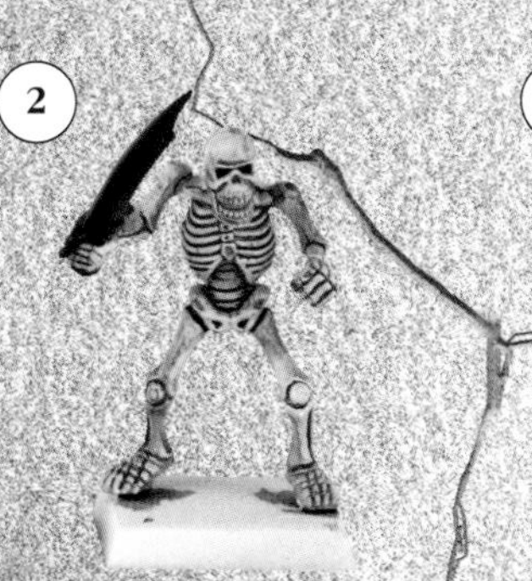

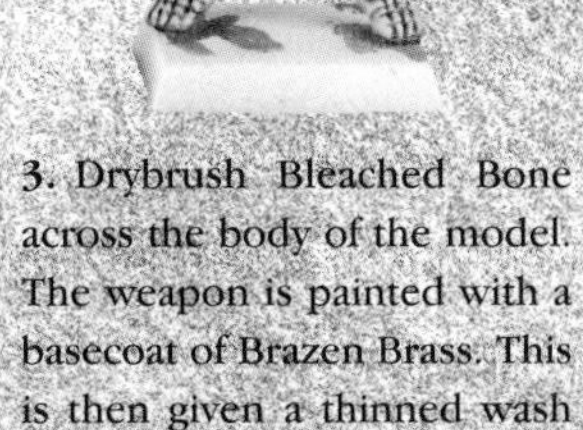

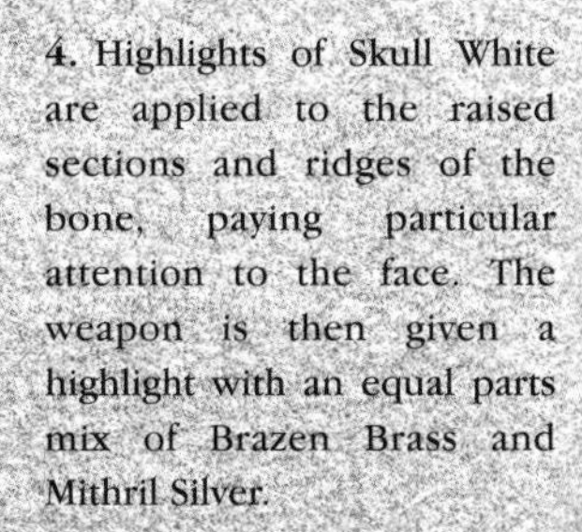

This is a more detailed method used by the 'Eavy Metal team to paint the Studio army.

1. Undercoat the model with Skull White.

2. Apply a wash of Brown Ink that has been thinned with an equal quantity of water. The weapons are then given another undercoat, this time with Chaos Black.

3. Drybrush Bleached Bone across the body of the model. The weapon is painted with a basecoat of Brazen Brass. This is then given a thinned wash with Chestnut Ink.

4. Highlights of Skull White are applied to the raised sections and ridges of the bone, paying particular attention to the face. The weapon is then given a highlight with an equal parts mix of Brazen Brass and Mithril Silver.

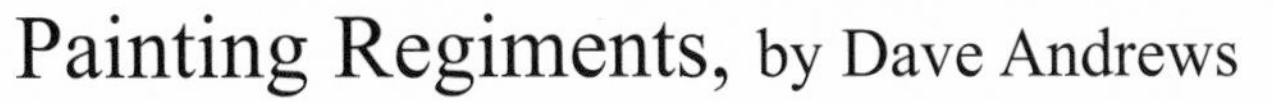

# Painting Regiments, by Dave Andrews

"I wanted to create an effective looking force but one that was quick to finish. To do this I painted every model in the army at the same time, applying a basecoat to each figure before moving on to the next colour or highlighting stage. The hieroglyphs on the scrolls and shields were photocopies from a source book which were then reduced, a simple but very effective technique."

"To paint the bone on my army I sprayed the models with a Chaos Black undercoat. Snakebite Leather was then painted over this, followed by a drybrush with Bubonic Brown. A drybrush of Bleached Bone was then applied. To finish the models, the teeth were picked out with Skull White."

# TOMB KINGS CAVALRY

We used the same method for painting the bone of our Skeletal Steeds as we used for the Skeleton Warriors. To make things easier, we chose to paint the steeds and the riders separately before they were glued together.

*Skeleton Heavy Horsemen*

*By applying a limited palette and contrasting colour scheme, combined with a very simple painting technique, Dave Andrews*

Chariots provide a great opportunity to add colour and variety to your army. We kept our turquoise theme on the details, but added an extra colour to the bodies of the chariots themselves. This deep red is achieved by basecoating with Scab Red and highlighting with Red Gore.

## Painting Gold

To paint the gold in our force we used a basecoat of Shining Gold. This was given a wash with Chestnut Ink, before highlights of Burnished Gold and Mithril Silver were applied.

*Skeleton Chariots*

*was able to paint a brilliant force in a very short space of time.*

# TOMB GUARD

*Tomb Guard Champion*

Although Tomb Guard wear more armour and decoration than other skeletons we decided to make this elite unit stand out even more. We painted the shields of our Tomb Guard with the same red scheme we had used on the chariots' bodies.

To complete the base of our models we glued sand to each one with PVA. Once this had dried a basecoat of Snakebite Leather was applied which was drybrushed with Bubonic Brown, followed by a final drybrush of Bleached Bone.

*Tomb Guard by Chris Frosin*

# CONSTRUCTS

**Undead Constructs are created using all manner of materials, so you might like to paint them as if they were made from bone, metal, stone or a mix of these.**

*Ushabti*

As the Ushabti are larger than most of the models in a Tomb Kings army, it is well worth spending some extra time and attention when painting them. Whilst the skull trophies and armour of the Ushabti have been painted in keeping with the theme of our army, their bodies are painted with Chaos Black, which is highlighted with Chaos Black mixed with increasing amounts of Bleached Bone.

*Bone Giants*

# TOMB SCORPIONS

To make our Tomb Scorpions look like they are made from all manner of materials as well as bone, one of the carapaces was painted to resemble black stone, while the scarab-like head was painted gold to add an element of decoration.

# TOMB SWARMS

*"It came from below..." Tomb Scorpions and Swarms attack an Imperial Mortar.*

# CARRION

The dark nature of the Carrion contrasts well with the bone of the skeletons. The muscles and sinew have a basecoat of Scorched Brown, which is then highlighted with Dwarf Flesh. The feathers are painted Chaos Black and drybrushed with Codex Grey.

# SCREAMING SKULL CATAPULT

*Screaming Skull Catapults prepare to fire their terrifying ammunition.*

# TOMB KINGS

*Settra the Almighty, Lord of Nebekhara, Ruler of the Sands, Holy Eagle of the Desert.*

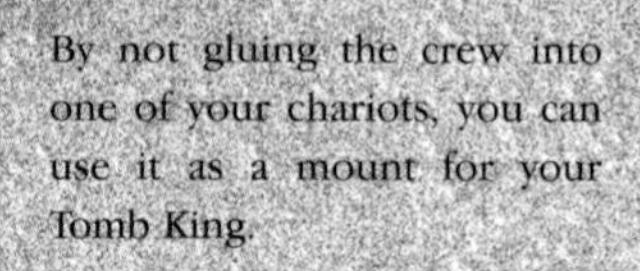

By not gluing the crew into one of your chariots, you can use it as a mount for your Tomb King.

*Tomb King*

Characters are important personages, and are represented by highly detailed miniatures. It is worth spending more time and taking more care on these figures, as a well-painted character can greatly enhance the overall look of an army. Our characters follow the unifying colour scheme of the army, with extra detail and highlighting to ensure that they stand out.

*Tomb King in Chariot*

# LICHE PRIESTS

Unlike Skeletons, Liche Priests still have ancient, withered skin. Ours are painted with Codex Grey, highlighted with Bleached Bone.

# CASKET OF SOULS

*A Liche Priest summons forth the dark powers that lie dormant within the casket.*

# BATTLEFIELDS OF NEHEKHARA

*The Studio Tomb Kings army in all its glory marches across our Nehekhara terrain.*

We created some specially themed terrain as the perfect complement to our army. If you can do this not only will it add to the overall look of your army but it will make your battles far more spectacular.

THE GLORIOUS CHARIOTS OF KING ALKHAZZAR I AT THE BATTLE OF THE GOLDEN SKULL.

# MIGHTY HEROES OF NEHEKHARA

*This page details some of the most powerful undead heroes of Nehekhara ever to have walked the Warhammer world. They may inspire you to create characters of your own devising for use in your games, which you can use with your opponent's consent.*

*On the pages that follow are rules and background for Settra, first and foremost of the Tomb Kings, and Khalida, Tomb Queen of the Eastern Deserts. These two characters may be included in your army and do not require your opponent's consent to include them.*

## King Phar

When Settra first began his domination of the Kings of Nehekhara he faced fierce resistance from rival kingdoms. Under his skilled generalship, Settra's armies were able to conquer all opposition before them, until they marched east through the Valley of the Kings. Word had spread of Settra's coming and one King was determined to defy this all conquering army. Under his rule the lands around Mahrak had been scoured clean of the greenskin menace and the city had prospered. An arrogant and proud leader, King Phar deemed himself too important to bow down before any mortal. He was able to ambush Settra's force as they marched through the Valley of the Kings, preventing the army from taking his beloved city.

For decades his people held out , besieged many times by the armies of Khemri and, even with his dying breath he cursed the name of Settra, remaining the only King who refused to pay him tribute. Finally, with Phar's passing, Settra's armies were able to conquer Mahrak and the last free city of Nehekhara fell under Settra's rule. Phar was among the first of the Kings to rise from his eternal slumber. Upon awaking, such was his fury that his successors had bowed down to the lineage of Khemri that he broke into the tombs of his descendants as they woke. Ordering their pyramids toppled, he dragged their mummified corpses from their resting places, burning them and shattering their charred skeletons with his mighty Flail of Skulls. Even in death, King Phar continues to fight against Settra, and his Undead legions wage war against all who try to subject him to their will.

## Sehenesmet, Vizier of Quatar

The tomb-city, Quatar, is famed for its towering statues, many of which are colossal representations of the gods and mighty kings of the past. Sehenesmet, the Vizier of Quatar, has worked for nearly a score of centuries creating, rebuilding and caring for these monoliths. Unmatched in this field, Sehenesmet has refined his incantations so that he can animate and control a great many of these constructs at any given time. It is he who inscribed the powerful incantations of awakening and binding upon the towering monoliths that guard the entrance to the famed Valley of the Kings, and his realm of walking statues is talked of in the lands of Araby in hushed tones. It has been said that he has even animated the great stone guardian of Quatar, shaped in a hybrid form of lion and eagle. Now it is even rumoured that he has interred himself within the animated body of a giant construct to lend him the strength so that he may undertake more ambitious and grander projects.

## Prince Tutankhanut

Prince Tutankhanut was the only son of the wealthy King Ahken of Numas and was famed throughout Nehekhara for his handsome features. Tragically, the young Prince was slain before he had even come of age at 15. He had been hunting lions, for he was renowned as a particularly skilled bowman, even when speeding along the plains on his war-chariot. Separated from his hunting party, a crude spear hurled by a savage northern tribesman smashed into his chest and threw him from his chariot. Adored by his wealthy father, Prince Tutankhanut was given an elaborate burial. When the young King awoke from his death sleep he was horrified at his withered skeletal form. According to the Nehekharan beliefs in the afterlife the gods would bestow each king with a body of gold. Tutankhanut was furious to find this was not the case and demanded that his priests fashion him such a body. When he arises from his tomb, resplendent in his golden body and death mask, the still living people of Numas hearken to his call, perceiving him as blessed by the gods. When the Prince and his army march to war the people join behind the icon of Tutankhanut, marching alongside their long dead ancestors to war. Tutankhanut has led his army to many victories. Fighting in the thick of battle his golden form deflects even the most powerful attacks.

# SETTRA THE IMPERISHABLE

*"And, behold, the almighty god-king Settra did awaken from his sleep of blessed oblivion. His legions, long buried beneath the sands, did arise and stand to attention, awaiting his order. And he did say 'War', and the world did tremble..."*

Of all the kings of Nehekhara, none could match the splendour, cruelty and arrogance of Settra, first Priest King of Khemri. Under his inspired leadership and unparalleled ruthlessness, the many kings of Nehekhara were conquered and forced to pay tribute and acknowledge Khemri as the greatest city of the land. The tribes of the surrounding lands were conquered and the armies of Settra spread far and wide, enslaving all before them. His war fleets ravaged realms across the sea, bringing the terror of the Priest King to many distant lands. Settra was a vain and egotistical king, demanding tribute and adoration from all his subjects and, though he was a tyrannical ruler, Khemri entered an unprecedented golden age of prosperity under his rule.

Settra's kingdom stretched across the land, but for all his conquests, he was unsatisfied, knowing that one day death would rob him of all he had accomplished. In his arrogance he vowed that the grave would not claim him and proclaimed that he would cheat death, setting his wisest and most powerful priests towards working on a means of preventing his passing.

The priests journeyed for many years throughout the world, searching for a means of keeping the great king from death, but to no avail. Great was Settra's wrath and though the priests' magic kept him alive far beyond his mortal span, they could not prevent his death. As he lay dying, the priests promised the great king that it would one day be possible for him to return from beyond the grave and live forever in a golden paradise where he would reign eternally. When the king died, it was with a curse on his lips and his body was taken to the great Pyramid of Khemri where he was entombed beneath the earth to await the appointed time for him to awaken.

But for the twisted ambition of the evil necromancer, Nagash, Settra's plans might have come to fruition. As Nagash's powerful spell coursed across the lands of Nehekhara, legions of warriors and kings from ancient times stirred and rose from their sepulchres. Where the ancient kings had been promised eternal life in a paradise where they would reign supreme, they instead awoke to find themselves clad in rotted vestments and desiccated flesh with their lands in ruins and kingdoms destroyed. The fires of pride and ambition still burned within their breasts and they set about reclaiming what remained of their kingdoms. Battles raged throughout Nehekhara until the great Pyramid of Khemri opened and Settra emerged into the blazing sunlight. Great was his fury at this disastrous reawakening and he set about reconquering his lost realm, overwhelming all those lesser kings who stood against him and forcing them to swear terrible oaths of fealty.

Having passed into the realm of death, Settra knew now that his priests had lied to him and kept much of their magic for themselves. His power was now far greater than theirs and he cast them from his lands, ordering his vassal kings to return to their tombs and await his call to arms. He would remain awake, king of a devastated land; ready to begin the reconquest of the empire that was once his. Immortality was now his, and the new races that had flourished in his absence would now feel his wrath.

# Settra – Tomb King of Khemri, Ruler of Nehekhara

*Settra was the first of the great kings of Nehekhara and remains the greatest of the Tomb Kings. He can be taken as one of your Lord choices in a Tomb Kings army. In addition, so powerful is he that he also uses up an additional Lord choice. He must be used exactly as presented here and may not be given any additional equipment or magic items. Settra must be the army general.*

| | M | WS | BS | S | T | W | I | A | Ld |
|---|---|---|---|---|---|---|---|---|---|
| Settra | 4 | 7 | 4 | 5 | 5 | 4 | 4 | 5 | 10 |
| Chariot | – | – | – | 5 | 5 | 5 | – | – | – |
| Skeletal Steed | 8 | 2 | – | 3 | – | – | 2 | 1 | – |

**Points:** 625

**Weapons:** The Blessed Blade of Ptra.

**Armour:** The Armour of Golden Magnificence.

**Unit:** Settra rides upon his massive Chariot of the Gods.

## SPECIAL RULES

**Undead**
Settra and his chariot follow all the rules for Tomb Kings Undead found on pages 20-21.

**Flammable**
Lord Settra has had his ancient body preserved through elaborate embalming ceremonies. He is Flammable.

**Settra the Great**
The greatest Tomb King in Nehekhara, a powerful Priest King in life and founder of the Mortuary Cult, Settra alone amongst the Tomb Kings knows the secrets of the Liche Priests and understands their language and incantations. As well as being general of the army, Settra is also the Hierophant, and can use incantations in the same manner as a Liche High Priest.

**Settra's Army**
Settra's army represents his personal guard, and half the points of the army must be spent on the following unit types: Chariots, Heavy Cavalry and Tomb Guard. It may not contain any Liche Priests.

**The Will of Settra**
One of the best generals and strategists to have ever lived, in life it was Settra's mastery on the battlefield that allowed him to conquer the other Nehekharan cities. In death, it is that same remarkable will and genius that moves his undying army. In addition to his Incantations, Settra also has a special version of "My Will Be Done!", which affects all Chariot, Heavy Cavalry and Tomb Guard units in his army. He may use "My Will Be Done!" once on each one of the listed units per Magic phase, regardless of range or number of such units. He must do this before using any Incantations and remember that Smiting and Urgency may only be used successfully once on a unit per Magic phase.

**The Curse of Settra**
Should Settra's mortal vessel be destroyed, it explodes into a ravening swarm of flesh-eating khepra beetles which bite and sting the enemy before flying back to his pyramid to slowly regain his immortal form. In addition to the normal Tomb King's Curse, if Settra is killed by any means, then every enemy unit within 2D6" suffers 2D6 Strength 2 hits (distributed as shooting hits).

**Chariot of the Gods**
Settra's chariot follows all of the rules for normal scythed chariots (ie, it is not a light chariot), and so does D6+1 impact hits. Settra may only join a chariot unit whilst mounted, and if he does so, the unit no longer counts as fast cavalry.

**Unit Strength**
Settra has a Unit Strength of 2. His chariot has a Unit Strength of 6. This means that in total, Settra and his chariot have a total unit Strength of 8!

## MAGIC ITEMS

### THE BLESSED BLADE OF PTRA

*Settra wields a weapon imbued with the power of the sun god. In battle, Settra strikes down his foes with dazzling flashes of light that blind the enemy and scorches their skin.*

Settra always strikes first in close combat, even if charged. If an enemy also has the ability to strike first, then they strike in normal Initiative order. If this is also equal, roll a dice to see who strikes first (re-roll ties). Keep track of the number of hits Settra scores with his weapon. After his attacks have been resolved, any enemy unit in base contact with Settra must take a Leadership test, with a negative modifier equal to the number of hits caused by Settra. If the test is passed, the enemy avert their gaze and suffer no ill effects. If the enemy fail the test then they are reduced to Weapon Skill 1 for the remainder of that combat round. If they roll double or more than their modified Leadership value then in addition to being reduced to Weapon Skill 1, the unit suffers D6 Strength 4 hits (distributed as shooting hits). For example, if Settra hits a unit with Leadership 7 three times, a Leadership test of 4 or less is no effect, a roll of 5 to 7 reduces them to Weapon Skill 1, and a roll of 8 or more means they also suffer hits.

### THE ARMOUR OF GOLDEN MAGNIFICENCE

*Settra wears a suit of age-old, kingly armour that was said to have been crafted and worn by the jackal god, Djaf, when he walked the land. It is impervious to the ravages of time, and nothing can tarnish this shining golden armour.*

Settra has a 2+ Armour saving throw. This saving throw is never modified to worse than a 4+, even if hit by an attack that normally allows no Armour save (such as a cannonball).

### THE CROWN OF NEHEKHARA

*The crown that Settra wears represents his kingship over the entire land, and incorporates several crowns in one. This crown carries with it the blessing of all the gods and goddesses of Nehekhara, and is topped with a golden cobra that rears and spits whenever enemies are near.*

Settra and his chariot benefit from a 4+ Ward save. In addition, Settra causes *terror* as described on pages 81-82 of the Warhammer rulebook.

# HIGH QUEEN KHALIDA NEFERHER

High Queen Khalida, the Warrior-Queen of Lybaras, was highly respected across all the lands of Nehekhara and adored by her subjects. Her intelligence, temper and bravery were as legendary as her beauty, as was her intense sense of honour and justice. Her reign was tragically short, cut down as she was in her prime. All of Nehekhara mourned her passing, for they knew she would have brought great glory to the empire.

Khalida was killed by her cousin Neferata, the Queen of Lahmia, in ritual combat during a great celebratory feast. The sensuously beautiful and alluring Queen of Lahmia had falsely accused Khalida of treason and attempts of assassination, and proclaimed these allegations loudly during a banquet feast. Khalida had risen to defend her honour, and in her anger had refused to nominate a champion, accepting the challenge personally. Neferata desired the death of Khalida, for the Warrior-Queen had grown suspicious of Neferata and her Lahmian court. Indeed Khalida was right to be suspicious, for Neferata had been studying the blasphemous texts of the sorcerer, Nagash, and had drunk from the cursed elixir of damnation – she had been reborn into a cursed existence, becoming the first of the vampires, and if Khalida was not silenced then the Lahmians' deadly secret would become known.

The two women fought before the shocked nobility, their blades weaving a delicate and deadly dance. Khalida was a skilled and powerful warrior, and yet she could not match the preternatural speed or unholy strength of Neferata. As she lay on the tiled floor, her blood flowing from a terrible wound in her stomach, Neferata sunk her sharp teeth into Khalida's neck, sucking deeply. Biting hard on her own tongue, the Queen of Lahmia placed her lips over Khalida's, and her vampiric blood flowed down the dying Queen's throat.

As the life began to leave her dying body, Khalida knew that the cursed blood now flowed through her veins. In desperation, she cried out to the gods to save her from the same abominable fate that had taken hold of Neferata. The Goddess of the Asp heard her pleas and appeared to the dying Queen in a divine vision. The blessing of the Goddess purified the vampiric taint from Khalida's veins even as it drained the remaining life from her. In sorrow she was borne back to Lybaras.

The priests and priestesses of the Asp Goddess undertook the burial of the Queen, for they recognised that the blessing of their divine mistress was upon her, even in death. Khalida was embalmed and placed in a seated position within a specially made reliquary within the temple of the blessed Asp in Lybaras. There she sits unmoving, her face concealed behind a beautiful death mask created in her likeness. In times of dire need, when her homeland is threatened, the power of the Asp Goddess infuses her ancient limbs. Gracefully, she rises from her seated position, and glides across the temple floor, commanding the doors to open with a delicate motion of her hand. Her flesh slowly starts to return to its former beauty, gradually becoming as pale and hard as pristine white marble.

As the embodiment of the Asp Goddess in full fury, a wave of pure terror rolls over those who look upon her. With divine energy flowing through her limbs, Queen Khalida brings war and death to any who threaten her realm.

# Khalida – Beloved of the Asp Goddess, Tomb Queen of the Eastern Deserts

*The revered Khalida can be taken as one of your Lord choices in a Tomb Kings army. She must be used exactly as presented here and may not be given any additional equipment or magic items.*

| | M | WS | BS | S | T | W | I | A | Ld |
|---|---|---|---|---|---|---|---|---|---|
| Khalida | 6 | 6 | 4 | 4 | 5 | 3 | 9 | 5 | 10 |

**Points:** 420

**Weapons & Equipment:** Hand weapon (talons), Venom Staff.

## SPECIAL RULES

**Undead**
Khalida follows all the rules for Tomb Kings Undead found on pages 20-21.

**Flammable**
Khalida's body has been preserved through elaborate embalming ceremonies involving sacred oils and unguents, so is Flammable.

**Incarnation of the Asp Goddess**
Potent venoms run through the veins of Khalida, flowing into her long talons. All attacks made by her count as magical attacks and Poisoned Attacks (see page 114 of the Warhammer rulebook), and she herself is immune to poison. In addition to this, any of her attacks that count as poisoned (so any 6s to hit), will inflict D3 wounds rather than 1 as well as wounding automatically.

The Queen moves with the swiftness of a striking asp, and will always strike first in combat, even if she was charged. If her opponent also has this ability, resolve their attacks in Initiative order.

**The Queen's Command**
Khalida may cast Horekhah's Incantation of Righteous Smiting once per Magic phase. It is automatically cast, and cannot be dispelled.

**Army of the Queen**
During her life, Queen Khalida's army relied heavily on her well-trained bowmen. An army that includes Khalida must contain at least one unit of Skeleton Warriors armed with bows.

**Blessing of the Asp**
Units of Skeletal Bowmen, Skeletal Light Horsemen and Chariots in an army that includes Queen Khalida may be given the Blessing of the Asp at the cost of +2 points per model. All shooting by these units count as Poisoned Attacks.

**Terror**
A horrific aura surrounds the High Queen, and she causes *terror* (see the Warhammer rulebook, p.81-82).

**Regeneration**
The power of the Goddess of the Asp runs through Queen Khalida, energising her limbs and healing her wounds so that she looks increasingly statue-like and is filled with unnatural beauty and allure. She has the Regeneration special rule as described on page 113 of the Warhammer rulebook.

**Curse of Queen Khalida**
Any model or unit responsible for the death of Queen Khalida (see the Tomb Kings' curse on pages 22-23) is affected by her curse on the dice roll of 4+. If affected, then roll a D6 for each model/unit, and on the dice roll of a 6, the model loses a wound that cannot be saved in any way (including Ward saves) nor Regenerated. Roll again at the start of each of your opponent's turns for the rest of the game, and they take a further wound on a roll of 6.

## MAGIC ITEM

**VENOM STAFF**
*This staff, shaped in the form of a striking asp, writhes as if alive and spits at its enemys with the anger and spite of the Asp Queen herself.*

**Bound Spell, Power Level 5**
The staff contains a Bound *magic missile* with a range of 24", causing 2D6 Strength 4 hits. If a unit takes any wounds from the staff, it may not move in its next Movement phase.

# INSCRIPTION ON THE GREAT OBELISK OF KHEMRI

*Thought to be a recount of King Settra's dying words, as translated by one Alun Gärtner.*

Hail to the mighty tomb guards who stand before me, you who will stand guardian at my tomb chamber for eternity! For I, Settra, Lord and First King of Khemri will awaken to command you in the paradise that awaits us! Hail to the Ushabti and the Sphinx who crouch beside the monuments of the king. Hail to the commanders of my legions of warriors, leading forth your regiments to join me in eternity. Fill the air with the sound of your worship! Your standards are pleasing to my sight and that of the gods! See how the sun god shines upon them. Remember them gleaming this day as you enter the darkness of the tomb. Fear not what we must do and think only of the glory that awaits me upon the Great Awakening.

Look upon my flesh, my warriors! Once I was a mighty warrior-king, destined to live the life of a god, yet my flesh withers upon my bones, my frail body succumbs to the ravages of time and soon death will claim me. But it shall not always be so. In strange aeons, even death may lose its grip and though I march to the tomb, I have the spirit of a king! And you also, yet you be but mere mortals, you have the invincible spirit of the army of Settra!

Turn your heads my soldiers, turn your heads and see the fair river Vitae. You will see it again when the world is ready to receive us and you reclaim that which is mine by right and by birth. We are the glory of Khemri and shall rise again to fulfil our manifest destiny of ruling this world.

Now make ready your weapons, my soldiers, for the time is at hand. Go forth, I command you, go forth in haste and march with your king into the darkness of the tomb. Make great the name of Settra and Khemri! The darkness draws near and there are great deeds that remain undone, enemies yet to crush and raptures yet to rejoice in. So as it is written, so shall it be done. I, Settra have proclaimed it and let none dare oppose my will.

# THE BARROW KINGS

Scattered throughout the Old World and beyond lie ancient cairns; the burial places of early kings and their most loyal warriors. They are the last remnants of an ancient people predating the coming of Sigmar. Little is known of them, for they did not record their histories in written form, relying on a tradition of storytelling. These barrows are mounds of earth piled over a tomb, usually accessed by a single entrance. They range greatly in size, and some of the largest can be seen on the skyline for many miles around. Macabre and superstitious stories surround these mounds, and those who live near them go out of their way not to walk in their shadow. Bedecked in bronze armour, rumours say that these ancient kings stride from their burial mounds in the darkness, their warriors, loyal beyond the grave, marching at their side. It is said that the ancient druids of these people, figures of particular power and authority within the society, still walk the earth, directing mysterious powers and incantations against those who would desecrate the ancient kings' resting places. Scattered throughout the wilder lands are towering statues, and though weather beaten and old, many of them still resemble the nature gods and spirits that were once worshipped. It is said that these megalithic statues arise on nights of the new and full moons to stalk the darkness at the whim of the ancient druids. Some have speculated that there appears to be some link between these people and the ancient Nehekharans, although scholars have thus far been unable to provide much evidence to prove this claim.

Mikel looked on as Heinrich closed a gloved hand on a dust-covered goblet. Raising it close to his eyes, Heinrich inspected the vessel, wiping grime from its surface. Apparently satisfied, Heinrich dropped it into the heavy leather satchel worn over his shoulder, and shuffled deeper into the crypt.

Mikel glanced around anxiously, his torch sending flickering shadows dancing over the walls, and he flinched at the movement. The light revealed all manner of strange carvings on the walls, swirling patterns that entranced the eye, and strange wide-eyed figures with decorative headdresses.

"I think we should go, Heinrich," Mikel whispered, wincing as the sound of his voice shattered the silence. He felt as though the weight of the earth piled above was pressing down on his chest. His breathing was ragged, and despite the chill, his face was wet with perspiration.

Heinrich snorted in derision, and bent to examine something on the floor.

"Get outside and keep watch then. But you aren't getting a full share of what I find."

Uncaring about what could be looted from the burial chamber, Mikel half ran down the long, thin corridor towards the welcome sight of the stars. Stepping from the cairn, he breathed in the cold air deeply, running a hand over his clammy forehead. Passing clouds hid the full moon for a moment, and shadows deepened. In the darkness there was movement, and Mikel's felt his heart skip a beat. From the other cairns, spread in a semi-circle around the largest of the burial mounds, came the sound of many slow, deliberate footfalls. Adorned in strange, ancient bronze armour, a parade of long-dead soldiers marched from the darkness of the crypts and arranged themselves into fighting formations. Strange totems were held by some of the skeletal soldiers, and others held silent bronze horns to fleshless lips. From one of the larger burial mounds a bronze chariot emerged, pulled by the horrific vision of a pair of horses, flesh long since having fallen from their bones. As one, the skeletal legion began their advance, moving creakingly towards Mikel, skeletal hands clutching ancient weapons. Footsteps sounded behind him.

"We ha-have t-to go, Heinrich," he stammered. Hearing no reply, Mikel turned.

Heinrich staggered into view, and Mikel let out a groan of horror. The skin on Heinrich's face was grey and lined, as if he had aged a decade in the brief moments since he saw him. Heinrich raised a wrinkled hand, nails long and curling, towards Mikel in a silent plea. A heavy bronze blade suddenly chopped into Heinrich's neck from behind him, nearly severing his head from his body. With a gurgling sigh he fell to the ground, blood fountaining from the terrible wound. Standing in the gloom was a mighty figure, bedecked in intricately carved, age-old bronze armour. No sound issued from Mikel's throat, though inside, his soul screamed. Staring into the empty sockets of the once great king, he got the distinct impression that a cold intelligence still resided within this being. Mikel remained silently screaming and unmoving, even as the first blades pierced his body. He dropped to the ground, to be trampled into the icy earth. Only then, with all evidence of the intruders gone, did the ancient warriors return to their cairns, to guard their abodes silently for the remainder of eternity.

Angestag 8th Plugzeit 2499 - My good friend Jacob has at long last returned to Altdorf. After meeting him for a few ales in the Red Lion tavern, he seemed very insistent on visiting the Magnus Museum this very night. I persuaded him that whatever it was he so desperately needed to see could wait until a more decent, and most definitely sober hour. My curiosity is now raised though, especially after he kept on ranting about the sarcophagus of the infant King Kaspeh. I have arranged with the curator for us to visit first thing in the morning.

Festag 9th - Incredible chance has fallen upon us. Upon entering the museum Jacob headed straight to the newly refurbished 'Wonders of Ancient Nehekhara display. He spent a good hour scrutinising the small casket of Kaspeh with meticulous detail. Barely able to control his excitement, he informed me that the khepra pattern inset on the lid of the sarcophagus matches exactly a drawing on an ancient parchment he recently acquired from Araby. He also had on his possession a stone ankh and claims it is the key to the tomb of Queen Rasut. I have promised to keep both items safe until his return in a month.

Backertag 13th - After days of cross-referencing the parchment and extensive research, I have discovered that Queen Rasut was in fact Kaspeh's mother.
How intriguing! I took Jacob's parchment to my good friend Alun Gärtner. He deciphered the ancient hieroglyphs and I am now in a state of total excitement. It would seem the key to unlocking the infant king's casket was placed in the burial chambers of his mother Queen Rasut. Not only does the parchment detail the exact whereabouts of her tomb, but also how to gain access with the keystone. It would seem that inside the pyramid there lies a khepra amulet which when fixed onto the lid of Kaspeh's sarcophagus will open the casket.

There are a number of references to certain rites that must be performed to enter the burial chamber safely, but these sections are somewhat confusing and tedious. I dare say they are nothing more than ancient superstitions from a culture long since dead.

Wellentag 18th - It would seem that our good friend Alun Gärtner is unable to hold his tongue. Yesterday Clarissa Lohft, a renowned collector of antiquities from Nuln but who I suspect is little more than a glorified treasure hunter, paid the museum a visit and questioned me at some length about where the items we have on display were discovered. I feel that she knows more than she is letting on. When I returned to my chambers I discovered that during my time in the company of Fraulein Lohft, my room had been ransacked and the Ankh key stolen.

Bezahltag 22nd - After many sleepless nights I have decided that this matter is too important to leave until Jacob's return. Booking myself and my servant Klaus passage from the port of Marienburg to the city of Al-Haikk, I have left instructions to Jacob as to the course of my actions. I can but hope that the next time I meet up with my good friend, together we shall unlock the secret wonders of the casket.

Wellentag 27th Sommerzeit - It has been months since I last saw dry land, and now that I stand upon it I wish it were not quite so dry. The sun here is intolerable and the stench of camels even worse. Within minutes of stepping on shore I learned exactly why Al-Haikk is known as the City of Thieves. Undaunted by the loss of my purse, I have been asking around about the location of the city of Khemri. It seems my questions have brought some unwarranted attention. A group of men swathed in black robes approached me. Calling themselves the Servants of the Dead, they informed me my life will be at risk should I continue in my quest. I can only assume Clarissa has discovered I am in Nehekhara and seeks to reach the pyramid without competition. This episode has only strengthened my belief in the expedition, and I shall set forth with all haste lest Fraulein Lohft arrives at the tomb before me.

Aubentag 28th – Klaus has managed to procure a guide to aid us in our quest. Tomorrow I venture into the vast desert with my guide Araf and his young nephew Suli. Today I instructed Klaus to buy provisions for our journey including a good sword and a broad-rimmed hat to keep off the sun. I also asked him to find me a whip, for by the manners of the local camels I feel it will prove useful.

Marktag 29th – As suspected, my camel named Aborinothus has proven to be a veritable monster. It has a permanent state of flatulence and only travels where he so chooses. I tried using the whip on the creature but it only served to aggravate the beast even more. I shall be glad when I am no longer forced to share its company and I little doubt the feeling is mutual.

Bezahltag 30th – Yesterday Aborinothus wandered away from my guides. At first I was unconcerned as the beast does this on a daily basis returning me around feeding time. This time our separation proved near fatal. Whilst traversing one of the many dunes that scatter this barren land, the sand before us suddenly erupted and from it burst a monstrous beast. I recognised it to be a new species of scorpion but it was as large as a farmer's cart and branded with strange hieroglyphs. The creature attacked us, great pincers snapping and its fearsome stinger jabbing within inches of my face. I can only be thankful that Aborinothus was such a fast runner, as its cowardly flight no doubt saved us both. When I told my guides of this incredible beast they merely shrugged. Perhaps they think I am imagining things in the heat of the sun. Perhaps they are right.

Angestag 9th Vorgheim – The small oasis we have stopped at seems like a veritable paradise compared to the harsh desert. It has been such a long time since I last saw any sight, other than the monotonous glare of the desert sands. Late in the afternoon Klaus made a remarkable discovery.
On the far side of the small, but most refreshing pool, he stumbled across an immense skeletal footprint. Although it certainly looked authentic, I can only guess it is the work of some Arabian prankster.

Festag 17th – It has been a week since I last wrote in my journal, but truly there is little of noteworthy mention, other than the constant heat of this accursed sun. This morning I spotted some large birds flying in the skies above our small group. As the afternoon wore on the foul creatures flew low above our heads. From this distance I could see that even the vultures have little to eat in these arid lands for they looked as though they were starved to the very bone. I hope that the sight of these carrion eaters is not a bad omen.

Aubentag 27th Nachgeheim– Travelling across this wilderness has seemed to take an eternity, but at long last I have spied my first pyramid. The pinnacle of a huge black monolith appeared on the horizon and the sun had nearly set before I noticed a second pyramid beside the massive construct. At the sight of the black pyramid my guides made gestures to ward off evil. It confirms my beliefs that they are a superstitious civilisation indeed. For me the sight of this awesome tomb is indeed good news, for it means the destination of my journey is within sight and I can at last be free of my camel.

Bezahltag 5th – We have made camp in the old city. Tonight as the sun sets and the intolerable heat has dissipated, I will make my way to the tomb. According to Jacob's rough map the pyramid I seek lies exactly a mile to the south-east of the great tomb of Settra. The parchment shows a number of tombs located on the site, but how difficult can it be to locate a construction as large as a pyramid?

Festag 9th – I don't believe it! How many of these damned pyramids did the people of this ancient civilisation build? There must be hundreds of the accursed tombs At long last, after countless hours studying Jacob's parchment, and three frustrating days wandering the labyrinth of streets, we have found the one we seek. As I suspected Clarrisa has arrived before me, for the doorway lay open. Why I tremble so at the thought of entering the tomb I know not. As my mother always said, only fear the living for the dead are at rest. I shall endeavour to make notes in my journal. What marvels lie before me I can but wonder but it is my duty to record and map out these matters for posterity's sake.

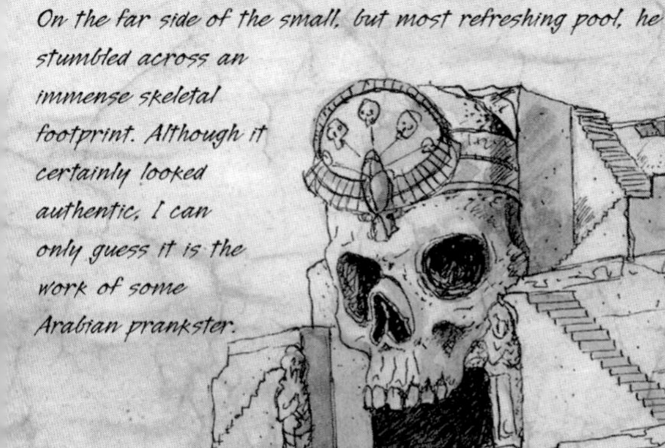

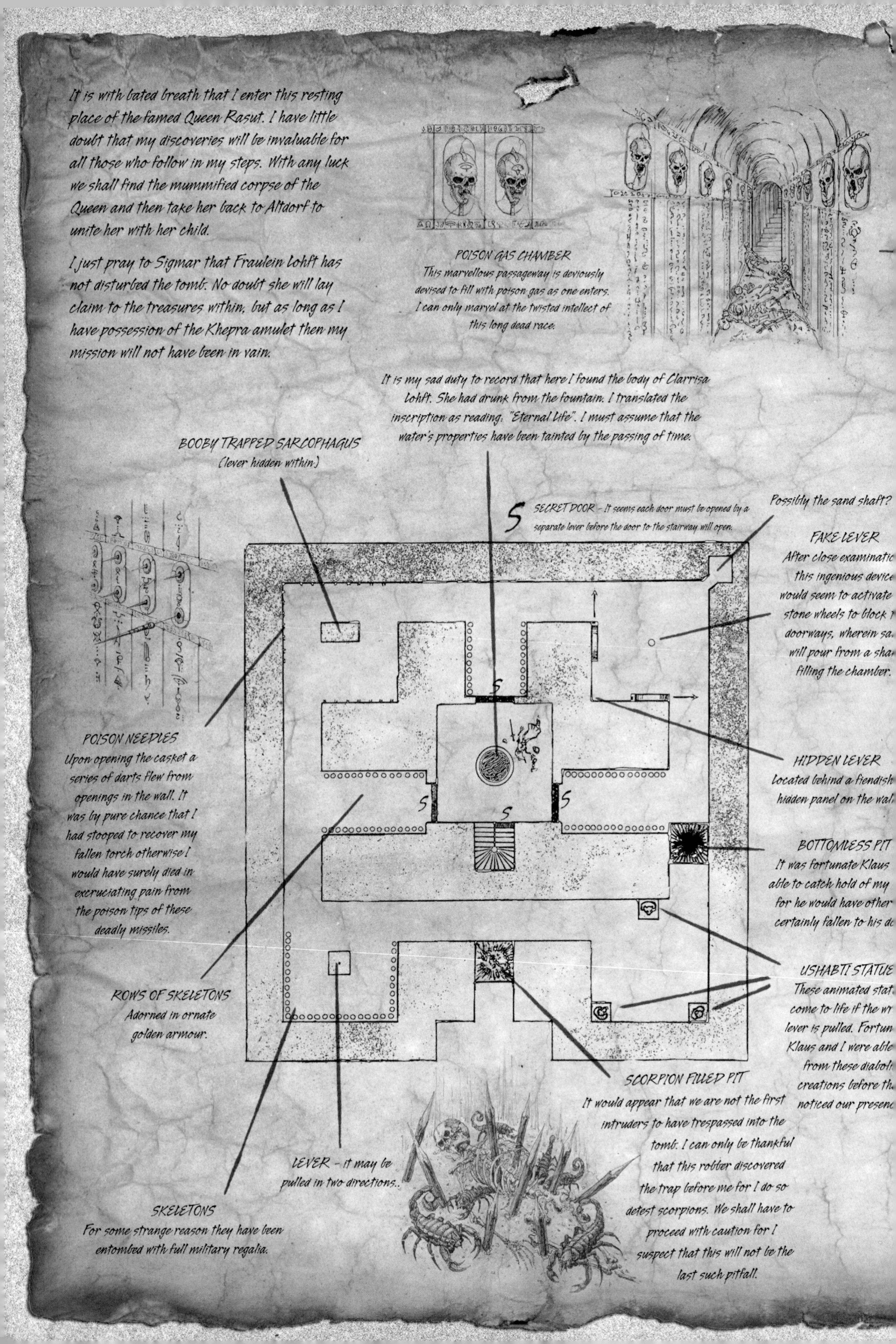
It is with bated breath that I enter this resting place of the famed Queen Rasut. I have little doubt that my discoveries will be invaluable for all those who follow in my steps. With any luck we shall find the mummified corpse of the Queen and then take her back to Altdorf to unite her with her child.
I just pray to Sigmar that Fraulein Lohft has not disturbed the tomb. No doubt she will lay claim to the treasures within, but as long as I have possession of the Khepra amulet then my mission will not have been in vain.
POISON GAS CHAMBER
This marvellous passageway is deviously devised to fill with poison gas as one enters. I can only marvel at the twisted intellect of this long dead race.
It is my sad duty to record that here I found the body of Clarrisa Lohft. She had drunk from the fountain. I translated the inscription as reading: "Eternal Life". I must assume that the water's properties have been tainted by the passing of time.
BOOBY TRAPPED SARCOPHAGUS
(lever hidden within)
SECRET DOOR - It seems each door must be opened by a separate lever before the door to the stairway will open.
Possibly the sand shaft?
FAKE LEVER
After close examinatio
this ingenious device
would seem to activate
stone wheels to block
doorways, wherein sa
will pour from a sha
filling the chamber.
POISON NEEDLES
Upon opening the casket a series of darts flew from openings in the wall. It was by pure chance that I had stooped to recover my fallen torch otherwise I would have surely died in excruciating pain from the poison tips of these deadly missiles.
HIDDEN LEVER
Located behind a fiendish
hidden panel on the wal
BOTTOMLESS PIT
It was fortunate Klaus
able to catch hold of my
for he would have other
certainly fallen to his de
USHABTI STATUE
These animated stat
come to life if the w
lever is pulled. Fortun
Klaus and I were able
from these diaboli
creations before th
noticed our presen
ROWS OF SKELETONS
Adorned in ornate golden armour.
SCORPION FILLED PIT
It would appear that we are not the first intruders to have trespassed into the tomb. I can only be thankful that this robber discovered the trap before me for I do so detest scorpions. We shall have to proceed with caution for I suspect that this will not be the last such pitfall.
LEVER - it may be pulled in two directions..
SKELETONS
For some strange reason they have been entombed with full military regalia.

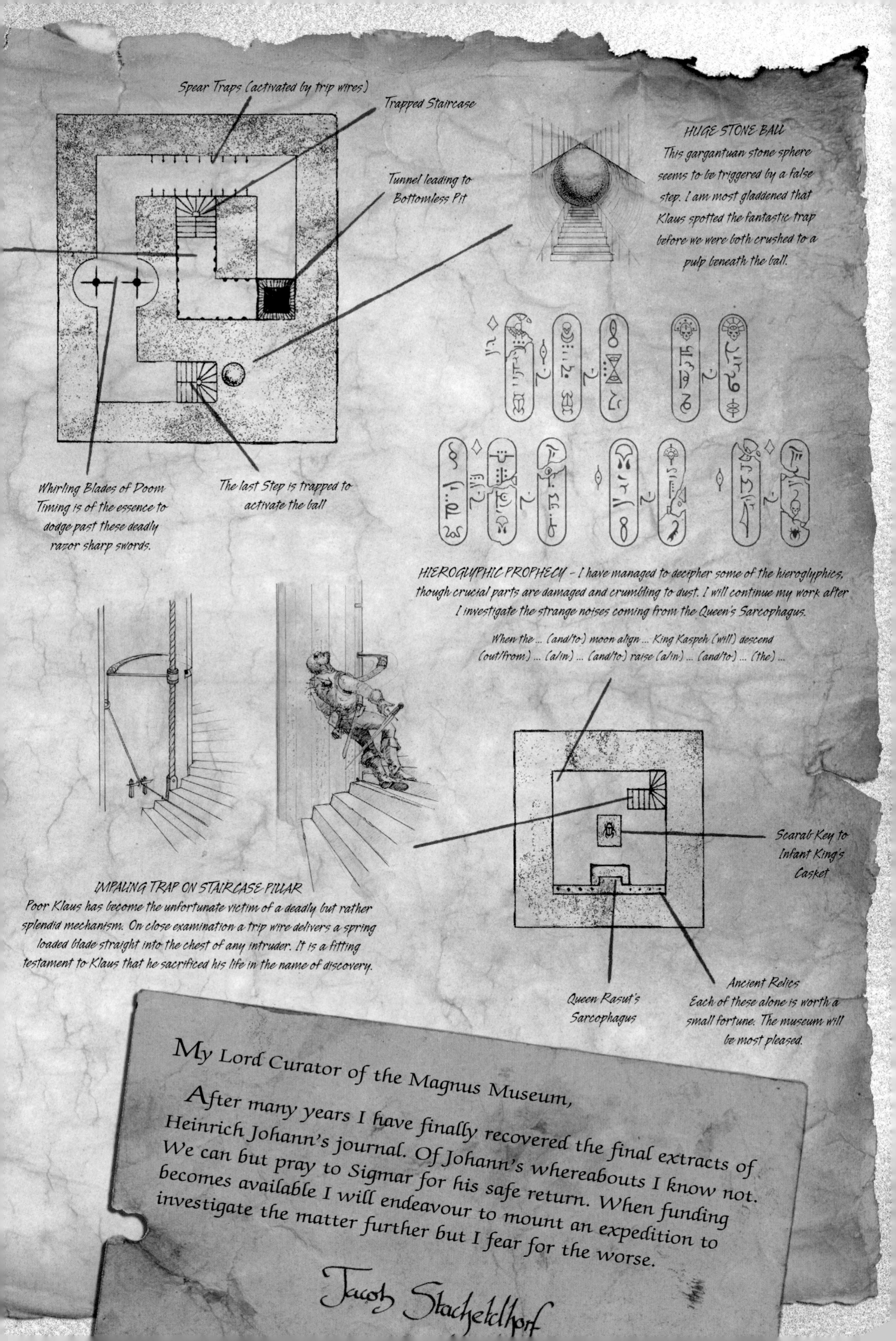
Spear Traps (activated by trip wires)
Trapped Staircase
Tunnel leading to Bottomless Pit
HUGE STONE BALL
This gargantuan stone sphere seems to be triggered by a false step. I am most gladdened that Klaus spotted the fantastic trap before we were both crushed to a pulp beneath the ball.
Whirling Blades of Doom
Timing is of the essence to dodge past these deadly razor sharp swords.
The last Step is trapped to activate the ball
HIEROGLYPHIC PROPHECY - I have managed to decipher some of the hieroglyphics, though crucial parts are damaged and crumbling to dust. I will continue my work after I investigate the strange noises coming from the Queen's Sarcophagus.
When the ... (and/to) moon align ... King Kaspeh (will) descend (out/from) ... (a/in) ... (and/to) raise (a/in) ... (and/to) ... (the) ...
IMPALING TRAP ON STAIRCASE PILLAR
Poor Klaus has become the unfortunate victim of a deadly but rather splendid mechanism. On close examination a trip wire delivers a spring loaded blade straight into the chest of any intruder. It is a fitting testament to Klaus that he sacrificed his life in the name of discovery.
Scarab Key to Infant King's Casket
Queen Rasut's Sarcophagus
Ancient Relics
Each of these alone is worth a small fortune. The museum will be most pleased.
My Lord Curator of the Magnus Museum,
After many years I have finally recovered the final extracts of Heinrich Johann's journal. Of Johann's whereabouts I know not. We can but pray to Sigmar for his safe return. When funding becomes available I will endeavour to mount an expedition to investigate the matter further but I fear for the worse.
Jacob Stacheldhorf

# ARISE AND RECLAIM YOUR EMPIRES…

Nehekhara was once a powerful and proud nation. Tragically, through the blasphemous magic of the cursed sorcerer Nagash, the entire population was slain. Now the Nehekharans are more powerful than ever – every one of their warriors that was entombed over the centuries can march to war, and their Tomb Kings are as proud, noble and arrogant as ever. Dead soldiers also don't run away, and scare the pants off their opponents – so it's not all bad…

We have designed the Tomb Kings army so that it conveys the relentless nature of the Tomb Kings themselves. This is an army that has been around for thousands of years, long before the rise of the Empire – and they have got a few things right over this length of time! It can be a really intimidating force to face because they are so unyielding – you know they're not going to run away, you know they can advance and shoot you without penalties and you know that they can potentially throw enough incantations around that you cannot stop them all. With practice and good tactics, the Tomb Kings army can seem unstoppable. However, make a few untimely mistakes and the army will quickly begin to crumble around you.

## The Army of Eternity

The characters in the Tomb Kings army are vital to the army's success – after all, the army is standing only due to the incantations of the Liche Priests and the formidable will of the Tomb Kings and Princes. This is the way the army list has been designed – so don't be shy of using all the magical items and incantations at your disposal – that is what they are meant to be there for! Always protect your Hierophant – if he dies, your army will soon start to fall apart.

The Undead troops at your disposal are solid, but most of them are not the strongest or most skilful soldiers in the Warhammer world – they are dead after all. However, they are totally reliable – you can almost guarantee how they will fare in each game. They are not going to run away and even though you might take lots of casualties, you can always raise them back with incantations. Also, never underestimate the benefits of *fear* – remember that *fear*-causing units work best when they are deployed as large units, because if you beat an enemy in combat and outnumber them, they automatically flee.

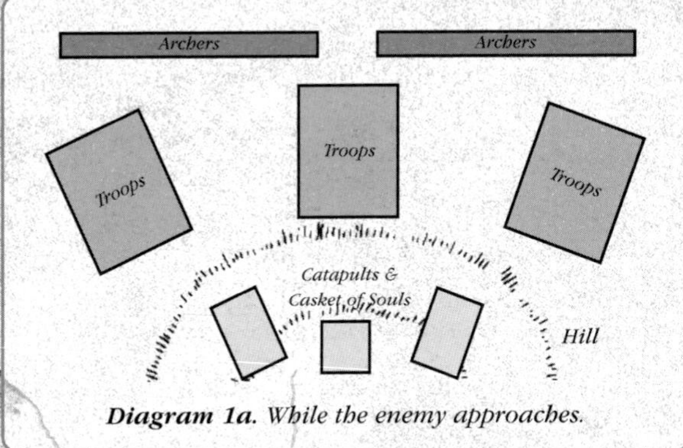


**Diagram 1a.** *While the enemy approaches.*

Foot Troops

Chariots, Cavalry & Carrion

**Diagram 2a.** *Refused Flank.*

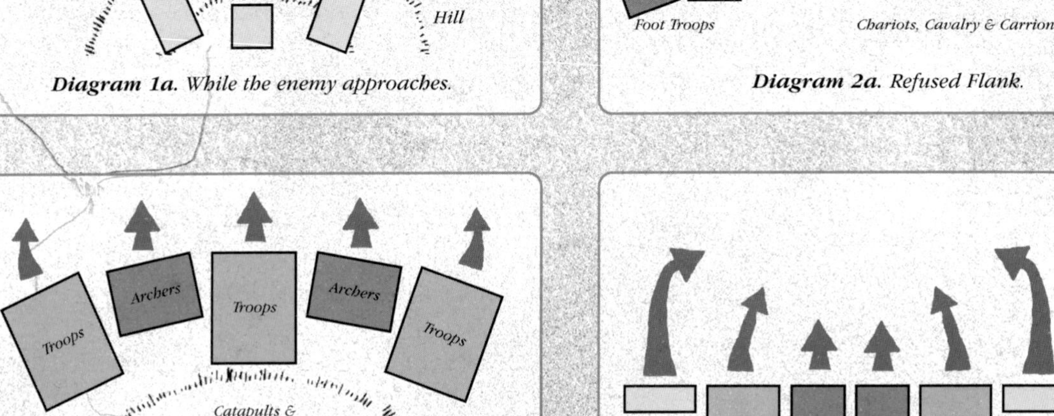


**Diagram 1b.** *When the enemy is close, reform into solid fighting blocks & attack!*

**Diagram 2b.** *Fast Cavalry Flank Attack.*

The constructs in the army (Ushabti, Tomb Scorpions and the Bone Giant) are powerful additions to the force, and are the things (along with your Tomb Kings and Princes) that can hit the enemy hard. They are also particularly resilient to taking damage – and if they are near an Icon Bearer they become even more so. Nevertheless, they are best used in a supporting role with your larger units.

Tomb Scorpions, Tomb Swarms and Carrion can be used to threaten enemy war machines and really mess up your opponent's tactics. Tomb Swarms are great to hold up expensive enemy units until you can bring other regiments to support them. Even just the threat of having units arriving in the middle of the battlefield can really distract your opponent from his battle plan.

# Tactics

Here are a couple of suggestions for tactics when using the Tomb Kings, and two main ways that the army can be used. They are fairly opposite in nature, but both are well worth trying out. After a few games, you might find that one suits the way you play better, or that a mix of the two works well.

## "And Let The Heavens Be Darkened With Arrows!"

This defensive tactic works really well if there is a hill for you to anchor your defence around (see Diagram 1a). Even without an anchor like this, it can still be an effective tactic by forming your own firebase.

The basic idea of this tactic is to have a solid centre of Skeleton Warriors with bows, as well as a Screaming Skull Catapult or two and/or a Casket of Souls. Your opponent will have to come towards you, or else get filled with arrows and have wailing, severed heads landing in their midst – not a comforting idea. This is when having the Casket comes in useful – the enemy really has to advance, meaning that his troops are going to be looking straight at the Casket itself – not the greatest position to be in!

On your flanks (even just behind your lines of archers) you will need some hard-hitting troops – your chariots, cavalry and Ushabti. Sit back and pepper your enemy with bowfire. Despite a Ballistic Skill of 2, always hitting on 5s can be devastating, especially in large numbers.

Use your characters to get your soldiers to shoot again in the Magic phase if you can – the more shots the better. Also, try to get Horekhah's Incantation of Righteous Smiting working on your Screaming Skull Catapults. By doing this, you can have them shooting twice in the one turn – and you can use this extra round of shooting to work out the range of your target so that in your Shooting phase it can be spot on target.

it;s a good idea to make your skeleton archer units quite large with a full command group of Standard Bearer, Musician and Champion. Once the enemy is close enough, just reform the unit, and it suddenly becomes an unbreakable fighting unit that is perfectly capable of holding up almost any enemy until support arrives.

After reforming your archers, it is time to move your supporting units on the flanks into position (see Diagram 1b). You either want to put them into a position so they can charge the enemy when they attack your archers, or into a good position to charge in the Magic phase. In this way, you can steal the initiative from your enemy and launch your own counter-attack at the most opportune time, hopefully hitting your foe in the flanks.

## "And The Ground Did Tremble As The King Marched To War!"

The all-out attack force works surprising well for what can at first seem like a very slow moving and unwieldy army. This is deceiving, for a magically-motivated army of the Tomb Kings can be surprisingly fast. Both Heavy and Light Horsemen are Core units, and if you take a Tomb King then Chariots are also a Core choice, and a refused flank tactic can work very well (see Diagram 2a). Always remember to use the ability of the Tomb Kings to shoot while moving forwards. Use your Magic phase to keep the army moving forwards as well as resurrecting any casualties. When the time is right, get ready to launch your units on the enemy, remembering that you can charge them in the Magic phase.

One good tactic (see Diagram 2b) is to get your fast cavalry (Light Horsemen and Chariots) into good positions (such as in place for flank charges) and then use the magic of your Liche Priests, Tomb Kings and Tomb Princes to charge them into the enemy at the right moment. This can work very well, but sometimes can be thwarted by the magical defences of your enemy – the best way to get it working is to practise your timing by playing games and experimenting with the number of Liche Priests and magical items in your army to find what works best for you. Knowing the right time to use the different incantations is vitally important in a Tomb Kings army.

If there is one vital charge that you need to get off, make sure that your characters are in a position that they can all try and make their incantation work through attrition – there is only so many Dispel dice that the enemy has!

To round off, here are a few points to remember:

Be relentless and tactical in your Movement and Magic phases – think ahead – make sure you position your characters in the right place so they can use their incantations to full effect in the Magic phase – remember that the incantations are fairly short-ranged.

Support your units. With the possible exception of Ushabti and Tomb Guard, most of the units in the Tomb Kings army will begin to fall apart against decent troops. Try to get your units attacking at the same time, rather than piecemeal. Use your fast moving units to support your infantry, hitting them in the rear and flanks, and have everything attack in one almighty charge!

Be cunning. The Tomb Kings is a great list for trying out tricks and sly tactics – make good use of your Magic phase to get extra phases of movement, use the range of useful magical items and banners and try out the various troops at your disposal. Most of all, have fun with them.

# Introduction to the Written Language of the Nehekharans

– As transcribed by the most scholarly Alun Gärtner –

The written form of the Nehekharan tongue (see Ch.4, pp IV for dialect entreaty) follows a highly organised and logical, if complex, grammatical structure. Even now, with my own study entering its fifth decade and several other notable if oftentimes disreputable scholars spending several years compiling deciphers and translations, there is still much that has thus far been impossible to interpret. Note: I use the term scholar in its loosest form, regarding the aforementioned rogues oft little more than opportunistic grave robbers – my own collection of artefacts (including a fully embalmed and remarkably well preserved ancient King) is a part of the great museum of Altdorf, free* for all to view and study. Below, I have provided the written forms of some of the most common words as a starting point to further reading and study. It would be wise to first learn these, as they will provide a good base from which to propel yourself into the world of this fascinating and dare I say exciting field. I will not endeavour to introduce the many and varied grammatical and thematic subtleties that alter the meaning of the interpretation at this point.

*I do not mean free literally of course. Entry fee varies, and is slightly more on religious festival days.

## Section 1.1: Nehekharan Hieroglyphics

I II III IV V VI VII VIII IX X XI XII

XIII XIV XV XVI XVII XVIII XIX XX XXI XXII XXIII XXIV

I, II, III. Sun / heart / soul
(same word or v. similar, possibly with different determinative to separate them?)

IV. The Great Desert

V. War

VI. Famine

VII. Eternal Life

VIII. Sand

IX. Nehekhara

X. Khemri

XI. Priest of the Gods

XII. Glory/Conquest

XIII. Vengeance

XIV. Damnation

XV. Serpent

XVI. The Underworld

XVII. The Heavens

XVIII. King

XIX. Army

XX. Loyalty

XXI. Necropolis / tomb

XXII. Water

XXIII. Warrior

XXIV. Foreigner
(literal translation "Uncouth Ones")

## Section 1.11: Translations

Here, I have included some of my own translations from various sources– I discovered that the lettering for the word 'enemies' is a combination of the Nehekharan words for 'damnation' and 'foreigners'. I also noted that the word for 'skies' is markedly similar to that used for 'the heavens'. It is my belief that this intriguingly infers that they believe their gods to dwell in the sky, even perhaps the stars themselves.

"And he did smite and destroy his enemies with great vengeance and furious anger..."

Translation from inscriptions in the tomb of King Amenemhetum of Zandri

"...and storms shall sunder the skies, and war will tear the world apart, and the dead shall rule the lands..."

From a heretical text written by an unknown Khemrian author

# BANNERS OF THE TOMB KINGS

Feel free to photocopy these banners for use on your own models. A good way to paint them is to use contrasting colours for the background and the image itself, as this makes the banner really stand out. For example, an image painted gold with a blue, black or red background works particularly well.

You could use these banners to represent unit standards or to represent a special magical banner carried by one of your elite units. You might like to use one of the larger banners for your army's Icon Bearer.

A small amount of converting is required to allow a Tomb Kings standard bearer model to carry one of the larger banners.

# REFERENCE

| Lords | M | WS | BS | S | T | W | I | A | Ld | |
|---|---|---|---|---|---|---|---|---|---|---|
| Tomb King | 4 | 6 | 4 | 5 | 5 | 4 | 3 | 4 | 10 | *Undead, Embalmed, The Curse, "My Will Be Done!"* |
| Liche High Priest | 4 | 3 | 3 | 3 | 3 | 3 | 2 | 1 | 9 | *Undead* |
| **Heroes** | **M** | **WS** | **BS** | **S** | **T** | **W** | **I** | **A** | **Ld** | |
| Tomb Prince | 4 | 5 | 4 | 4 | 5 | 3 | 3 | 3 | 9 | *Undead, Embalmed, The Curse, "My Will Be Done!"* |
| Icon Bearer | 4 | 4 | 3 | 4 | 4 | 2 | 3 | 2 | 8 | *Tomb Blades, Undead* |
| Liche Priest | 4 | 3 | 3 | 3 | 3 | 2 | 2 | 1 | 8 | *Undead* |
| **Core** | **M** | **WS** | **BS** | **S** | **T** | **W** | **I** | **A** | **Ld** | |
| Skeleton | 4 | 2 | 2 | 3 | 3 | 1 | 2 | 1 | 3 | *Undead* |
| Skeleton Champion | 4 | 2 | 2 | 3 | 3 | 1 | 2 | 2 | 3 | *Undead* |
| Skeleton Horseman | 4 | 2 | 2 | 3 | 3 | 1 | 2 | 1 | 5 | *Undead; Fast Cavalry* |
| Sk. Horseman Champ. | 4 | 2 | 2 | 3 | 3 | 1 | 2 | 2 | 5 | *Undead; Fast Cavalry* |
| Chariot | – | – | – | 4 | 4 | 3 | – | – | – | *Light Chariot, Undead; count as Special choice if army is led by a Tomb Prince* |
| Skeletal Steed | 8 | 2 | 0 | 3 | 3 | 1 | 2 | 1 | 5 | |
| Tomb Swarm | 4 | 3 | 0 | 2 | 2 | 5 | 1 | 5 | 10 | *Undead, Swarm, Small, Skirmishers, Poisoned Attacks, "It Came From Below..."* |
| **Special** | **M** | **WS** | **BS** | **S** | **T** | **W** | **I** | **A** | **Ld** | |
| Tomb Guard | 4 | 3 | 3 | 4 | 4 | 1 | 3 | 1 | 8 | *Tomb Blades, Undead* |
| Tomb Guard Champion | 4 | 3 | 3 | 4 | 4 | 1 | 3 | 2 | 8 | *Tomb Blades, Undead* |
| Ushabti | 5 | 4 | 0 | 6 | 4 | 3 | 3 | 3 | 10 | *Undead Constructs* |
| Carrion | 2 | 3 | 0 | 3 | 4 | 2 | 3 | 2 | 4 | *Flying unit, Undead* |
| Tomb Scorpion | 7 | 4 | 0 | 5 | 5 | 4 | 3 | 4 | 8 | *Undead Construct, "It Came From Below...", Poisoned Attacks, Killing Blow, Magic Resistance (1)* |
| **Rare** | **M** | **WS** | **BS** | **S** | **T** | **W** | **I** | **A** | **Ld** | |
| Screaming Skull Catapult | – | – | – | – | 7 | 3 | – | – | – | *Stone Thrower, Screaming Skulls, Undead, Skulls of the Foe* |
| Bone Giant | 6 | 3 | 0 | 6 | 5 | 6 | 1 | 4 | 8 | *Undead Construct, Large Target, Terror, Unstoppable Assault.* |
| Casket Guard | 4 | 3 | 3 | 4 | 4 | 1 | 3 | 2 | 8 | *Casket Guard: Undead, Tomb Blades, Casket of Souls: Terror, Light of Death, Spirit-Souls* |

## Tomb Kings Rules of Undeath

- All models in the army list are Undead.
- The army must include at least one Tomb King or Tomb Prince, who will be the army's General.
- The army must include at least one Liche Priest or High Priest who will be the army's Hierophant.
- If the Hierophant is destroyed, every friendly Undead unit, but not character, must take a Leadership test at the end of the phase, and at the beginning of every Undead turn thereafter. Every unit suffers a number of wounds equal to the amount the test is failed by. The General's or a Champion's Leadership may be used for this if appropriate.
- Undead are Unbreakable, but Undead units beaten in combat suffer one additional wound for every point they lose the combat by.
- Undead within 12" of their Battle Standard suffer one less wound than normal when defeated in combat.
- Undead are Immune to Psychology (see page 112 of the Warhammer rulebook).
- Undead cause *fear* (Warhammer rulebook, page 81).
- Undead cannot make a march move.
- Undead can only react to charges by holding.

## Nehekharan Incantations

- All magical effects must be performed in strict order:
  1. All bound items not used by characters.
  2. Icon Bearer: Bound items
  3. Tomb Princes: "My Will be Done!" and Bound items
  4. Tomb Kings: "My Will be Done!" and Bound items
  5. Hieratic Hierarchy – High liche Priest & Liche Priest Bound items and incantations.
  6. The Casket of Souls
- Liche Priests and High Priests generate no Power dice.
- Liche Priests generate 1 Dispel Dice, High Priests generate 2 Dispel dice.
- All Priests know all four Incantations. Liche Priests may cast one per turn; High Priests may cast two per turn.
- Power level is rolled for each incantation as it is cast; Power Level 2D6 for Priests' incantations, or 3D6 for High Priests' incantations.

### INCANTATIONS

**Incantation of Vengeance:** *Magic missile*; range 18"; D6 Strength 4 hits.

**Incantation of Righteous Smiting:** Target friendly Undead within 12". If not in close combat, unit may take extra Shooting phase immediately. If unit is in close combat, all models, including mounts, can make one close combat attack against models they are in base contact with. Units may be affected by this incantation only once per Magic phase

**Incantation of Summoning:** Target Undead within 12", even if engaged in combat. Unit regains D3 wounds (or D3 wounds worth of models). Tomb Guard regain D6 wounds worth of models rather than D3. Skeleton Warriors are easier to resurrect than other Undead, so two D6 may be rolled, and choose highest.

**Incantation of Urgency:** Target unit within 12" and not in combat may immediately make a normal move. Unit may charge and all normal charging rules apply. A unit charged by means of this incantation reacts as normal and must take the appropriate Psychology tests.Units may be affected by this incantation only once per Magic phase, regardless of its source.